C000139105

THE
SHOTGUN
History and Development

The Pape shotgun showing the striker retraction system and the extractor.

THE

SHOTGUN

History and Development

GEOFFREY BOOTHROYD

SAFARI PRESS, Inc.

P.O. BOX 3095, Long Beach, CA 90803

CAUTION!

This book contains information on old and new firearms that reflect the particular experiences of the author. The author writes of specific firearms, cartridges and other equipment used under conditions that are not necessarily reported in this book. Please use appropriate caution when shooting old (and new) firearms, always making sure that the proper cartridges are used. When in any doubt have your firearm inspected by a competent gunsmith before attempting to shoot it. The publisher can not accept responsibility for the data in this book.

THE SHOTGUN by Geoffrey Boothroyd.
Copyright © 1985 by Geoffrey Boothroyd. Published by arrangement with A & C Black Ltd., London. All rights reserved. No part of this book may be used or reproduced in any manner whatsoever without prior written permission from the publisher. All inquiries should be addressed to:
Safari Press, Inc., P.O. Box 3095, Long Beach, CA 90803, U.S.A.

Boothroyd, Geoffrey.

ISBN 940143-92-5

1993, Long Beach, California, U.S.A.

10 9 8 7 6 5 4 3 2 1

Readers wishing to receive the Safari Press catalog, featuring many fine books on big-game hunting, wingshooting, and firearms, should write the publisher at the address given above.

This is the 48th book published by Safari Press.

Contents

CONTENTS

About this book

I started writing for *The Shooting Times* in 1958. The first article I submitted was, to my surprise, published and I was paid eight guineas. This was the first money ever earned by writing and the pleasure of receiving payment for something I had enjoyed doing was exceeded only by the delight in seeing my words and photographs published. That was a quarter of a century ago and from that one article accepted by the then editor, Tim Sedgewick, has grown a special relationship with succeeding editors and staff and, of equal if not more importance to me, a quite remarkable relationship with the readers of the magazine worldwide.

I had been given a more or less free hand to write about anything I liked so that, in addition to the single article, which I submitted when I felt like writing, I also contributed several series, one of which, on the development of the shotgun, introduces the main body of this book.

In 1968 I was asked by Philip Brown, who by then had become editor, to write weekly articles; in fact, to become a "regular contributor". At first I refused, not from modesty but because I just couldn't see how I could sustain a weekly article, week in week out.

Philip, who was a wise old bird, told me that the series would be self-perpetuating and that the "feedback" from readers and from people in the trade would provide ample raw material on which to base the articles. This, in effect, is just what happened. The series dealt with "firearms" and covered shotguns, rifles, pistols, books, ammunition, tools and, of course, people. Emphasis was largely on the historical aspects of the subject and on the second half of the nineteenth century in particular.

Once the series got under way the reader response followed. Letters came from all sorts of people. Well over half posed queries, some of which I was able to answer. The remainder provided information, much unobtainable from any other source.

Information has come to me by letter, from visits to fellow enthusiasts, telephone calls, not only from the U.K. but from Europe, Canada and the U.S.A. and from visits to gunmakers here and abroad and to museums and libraries.

This book is mainly concerned with the sporting shotgun and its development. I understand from readers that many of them collected the articles in the series and these have been carefully kept. However, weekly magazines all too often come into the general class of ephemera, like gun catalogues, and are cast away when read. Even those which are saved suffer from deterioration and it was in response to the suggestion by many readers that a collection of some of the articles be brought together in a more permanent form that the two books on shotguns were assembled. It is widely accepted in the publishing business that books based on a collection of previously published articles are rarely successful. Because of this rather gloomy forecast I had thought of rewriting the articles in a different manner, using the facts and photographs in a new and different presentation. I was persuaded not to do this but to find a publisher who would agree to publish the articles more or less as they were. This I was most fortunate in being able to do; some editing has taken place, some corrections carried out and I have made an attempt to eliminate as much repetition as possible. However, because of the manner in which the articles were originally written and because of their original purpose some repetition is unavoidable. Please bear with this.

For the technically minded most of the photographs unless otherwise acknowledged in the text were taken by me, most of them with 35 mm cameras using Ilford FP4 and PanF film developed in Beutler "home made" brew. Some were taken with larger format cameras but far and away the majority were taken by Canon and Nikon cameras and Vivitar macro-lenses. Many were taken outdoors with a simple set-up at the various Game Fairs here in the U.K. where not only did I have the pleasure of meeting readers but also having the opportunity of photographing the guns they kindly brought for me to see.

So, my thanks go first of all to the readers of *The Shooting Times*, past and present: I cannot name them all personally since the list would be longer than the book! My thanks to the editors and staff of *The Shooting Times* for publishing the material in the first place and agreeing to its re-publication in book form. I would also like to thank Chris Brunker of Christie's and James Booth of Sotheby's for their unstinting help and my many friends in the gun trade: I would single out two, the late Harry Lawrence of James Purdey & Sons and Len Onions of Bailons Gunmakers Ltd. of Birmingham. Without the help of my old friend W. A. C. Paton the task of putting these two books together would have been far more difficult and I have to thank my wife Nancy for proof reading and Jean Bayfield who did the typing.

Glasgow, 1985

I

A Brief History

A seventeenth-century wildfowling scene. Illustrated is the stalking
horse and the use of nets. Note also the caged decoy.

EARLY HISTORY

That is ever esteemed the best fowling-piece which hath the longest barrel, being five ft and a half or six ft long, with an indifferent bore, under Harquebuss. Provide the best sort of powder as near as you can, and let it not be old, for keeping weakens it much, especially if it grow damp: therefore, when you have occasion to use it, dry it well in a Fireshovel and sift it through a searcher to take away that dust which hindreth the more forcible effects and fouleth your piece. Let your shot be well sized and of moderate bigness; for if it be too great then it scatters too much; if too small it hath not the weight nor strength sufficient to do execution on a large fowl.

This is the brief advice contained in the chapter on "The Fowling-Piece and the Stalking-Horse" in the fourth edition of *The Gentleman's Recreation* published in 1697.

The earliest English sporting work to which reference was made of shooting was the classic treatise by Gervase Markham, *Hunger's Prevention, or the Whole Art of Fowling* published in 1621. However, in the *Merry Wives of Windsor* which was written in 1597 Master Ford is described as being out "a 'birding", but regrettably we learn little of the type of weapon employed or the technique of birding. We are told about Master Ford's amusing habit of discharging his birding-piece up the chimney on his return home, a somewhat wasteful method of unloading!

During the sixteenth and most of the seventeenth century, fowling was done with nets, "springes" or snares and with bird lime. When guns were used it was common practice to employ a stalking horse, specially trained for the purpose. In the absence of a live beast one could be made from old canvas, portable enough to permit it to be handled with one hand. When the birds had got wary of the horse "then you may stalk with an Ox or Cow, till the Stalking-Horse be forgotten, and by this means make your sport lasting and continual". Trees and bushes could also be employed, again made from painted canvas if the natural cover were insufficient.

The taking of both land and water fowl during this period was not so much a sport or pastime but rather a necessary means of augmenting the winter diet and the use of the birding-piece was incidental to the time honoured craft or profession of fowling by means of nets, snares, decoys and bird lime.

Since the birds were stalked and shot on the ground there was little incentive to modify or improve the weapons employed. In fact the only major change which took place was to substitute the flint and steel lock for the matchlock and so eliminate the annoyance of having to light the match and ensure that it was properly burning before taking a shot.

The early seventeenth century fowling piece was of 16-bore with a barrel up to six feet in length. The breech, octagonal in form, would be strongly reinforced and the

Opposite
The Gentleman's Recreation, the fourth edition published in London in 1697.

THE
GENTLEMAN'S
Recreation:
OF
FOWLING:
With a short Account of
Singing-Birds.

What Fowling *is* ; *with the Nature and Diversity of all manner of* Fowl.

FOWLING is used two manner of ways: either by Enchantment, or Enticement ; by winning or wooing the Fowl unto you by Pipe, Whistle, or Call ; or else by Engine, which unawares surprizeth them.

Fowl are of divers sorts, which alter in their nature as their Feathers ; but by reason of their multiplicity, I shall for brevity-sake distinguish them onely into two kinds, Land and Water-Fowl.

stock carried right up to the muzzle. The weight might be anywhere between 12 to 16 pounds and although ideally suited to burn a large charge of coarse powder, its weight and length made it impossible for it to be used against flying game.

It was not until the Restoration of the Monarchy under Charles II that the art of shooting flying game truly became a sport. The returning exiles brought with them sporting French flintlocks of the highest quality and spurred by example and necessity the British gunmaker sought to surpass his French rivals and, in fact, by the early nineteenth century succeeded in so doing. The eighteenth century was a period of consolidation, of careful attention to detail, and of greatly improved workmanship.

Detail improvements were made to the lock mechanism; the axle or tumbler on which the cock was pivoted was provided with an additional internal bearing or bridle as was the combined pan cover and steel. These improvements served to reduce the lock time contributing as they did to a reduction in friction and increased sweetness of operation. Towards the end of the eighteenth century a small roller was introduced between the feather spring and the toe of the pan cover and steel which materially increased the speed of operation of the lock and also the certainty of fire. Yet another source of friction was the bearing of the mainspring on the tumbler and the addition of a link or swivel connecting the mainspring and tumbler was another factor increasing efficiency of the lockwork.

All these improvements contributing to speed and certainty of fire increased the satisfaction of the sportsman of the eighteenth century. He had enough troubles to contend with without the additional annoyances imposed by a defective or sluggish mechanism, encumbered as he was by powder flask, shot flask or shot belt, wads, flints, turnscrews and vent pricker and in damp or wet weather vexed by misfires due to damp priming. This latter difficulty was alleviated, though not cured, by improvements in the design of the priming pan. The common pan would appear to have been especially designed to direct rainwater into the priming, and the "waterproof" pan did attempt to reduce this nuisance by the provision of a drain hole between the fence and the pan.

The greatest and most significant improvement is one which is not readily apparent by casual external observation. This was Henry Nock's patent breech which appeared in 1787. The common practice of closing the breech end of a gun had been to screw in a plug. Just ahead of the plug a hole was bored through the side of the barrel, the vent, which communicated the flash from the pan to the charge. Improved ignition of the charge had been obtained by the substitution of the "chamber breaching" for the common breech plug and whilst a chambered gun shot harder than one with a common breeching the time between the ignition of the priming and the ignition of the charge was unfortunately increased. This was due to the longer touch hole and Nock's invention eliminated this delay. At the end of the eighteenth century improvements in the mechanism of the lock, in the breeching and in the higher quality of craftsmanship

Opposite

Double flintlock shotgun by Ross of Edinburgh. Barrel length is 29¼″ and weight 8 lb. Note the waterproof pans, roller bearings on the "hammers" and cam surface on the feather springs.

available set the stage for the grand entry of the English double barrel sporting flintlock, the culmination of centuries of effort, the flintlock finally perfected.

THE FLINTLOCK PERFECTED

In the opening years of the nineteenth century the improvements in firearms had been such that the advice to the sportsman had been rather modified.

The fowling-piece which I should recommend is one with a stub twisted barrel, patent breech, platina or gold touch-hole, and to a person who is in the habit of shooting below the mark, an elevated breech; the length of the barrel from 26 to 28 in. As to who is the best gunsmith, it is a question, if an individual must be selected, of no easy solution. There are many country gunsmiths that make excellent fowling-pieces; but the London guns are certainly turned out in the best manner. Manton has obtained the highest celebrity, and justly merits much of the praise that has been bestowed upon him; but to rank him as the very pinnacle of excellence, unattainable by any other person, which has been attempted, is going too far. I am not decrying the work of Manton; on the contrary, I am willing to give him his due share of praise. Assuredly, he has acquired a name, of the importance of which he seems to be fully aware – for it brings him much business and enables him to charge a higher price than his fellow-labourers. However –

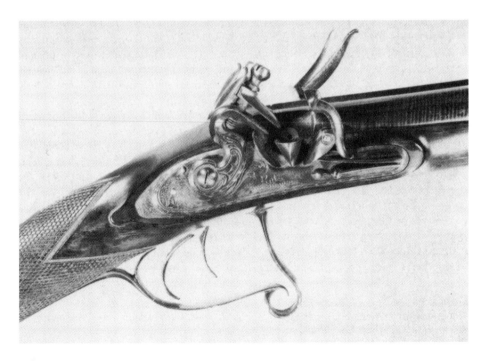

Mortimer sounds just as well in my ears as Manton, Knox as Mortimer, Gulley as Knox, Parker as Gulley etc., these are all esteemed manufacturers, and have alike sent forth guns of first rate excellence.

This, probably the most objective view of the contemporary scene, was written by Thomas B. Johnson in his *Shooter's Guide or Complete Sportsmen's Companion*, published in 1816.

What is not apparent is that there were two Mantons. John, the elder brother was born in 1752, Joseph, the younger brother born in 1766. The elder brother was usually referred to as Mr. Manton, the younger brother as Joseph Manton. John signed his guns Manton–London and later John Manton & Son, Joseph used his full name,

Double flint gun by John Manton c. 1825.
Weight 6¼ lb., barrel length 32″. Patent
breechings and the Manton "short"
lockplate. A "Dover Street" gun.

Joseph Manton, London. A far more eulogistic author was Peter William Lanoe Hawker who wrote the famous book on shooting, *Instructions To Young Sportsmen In All That Relates To Guns And Shooting*. First published in 1814 it ran to eleven editions and whilst John receives mention, it is brother Joseph who is praised. John's guns cost 50 guineas, Joe's 60 guineas in 1816. In the fourth and fifth editions of Hawker's work the inflationary spiral seems to have set in since the charges are now 55 and 65 guineas (1826). In the 1826 edition Mr. Purdey is mentioned as charging 55 guineas for his guns and in the sixth edition of 1830 Hawker records that "John Manton & Son carry on business in the best possible manner but Mr. Purdey has, at this moment the first business in London". Joseph had encountered severe financial difficulties and his business had closed down, and Hawker remarks "the London

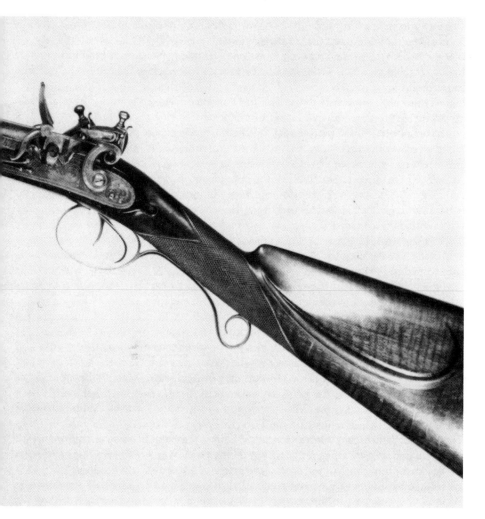

Gunmakers are now like frogs without a king" but the king was never able to regain his crown and he died intestate in 1835. John Manton, the less flamboyant brother, died in the previous year but his business continued until 1878.

More has been written about the Mantons than about any other sporting gunmaker. There is not the space to attempt an analysis of the relative merits of the two brothers but it can be said without fear of contradiction that their contribution to the art of gunmaking was incalculable. Not particularly because of their inventions, some of which were frivolous, but because of the extremely high standards which they set, standards which were impressed upon their workmen, an astonishing number of whom were themselves to found businesses.

The guns made by the Mantons were undeniably excellent above all in their proportions and in the restrained decoration. They established the style of the English sporting gun which has been emulated throughout the world.

As an example we can take a "Dover Street" John Manton & Son double gun of about 1825. This gun is typical of the design and styling at the end of the flint period. The overall length of the lockplate is shorter than before since the tail of the sear has been curved upwards, the so-called vertical sear, patented in 1821. The earlier "V" shaped pans have given way to the "U" or rounded dovetailed pans and as one would expect there is a larger roller bearing on the feather spring.

To the modern eye the provincial flintlock double gun appears to be excessively broad across the breech. By using the patent breech and almost "inletting" the lockplates into the breeching, the Mantons greatly reduced the overall width of the gun whch contributed greatly to its appearance and had the practical advantages of reducing the ignition time. The John Manton flintlock guns were also very strongly constructed. The single screw which secures the lockplates can be seen immediately behind the pan. This screw passes through a hole in the breeching instead of merely through the wooden stock.

The guns made by either of the Mantons are a delight to handle and once the eye is accustomed to the "top hamper" of flint, cock and steel and particularly if they can be used for a day in the field, the modern hammerless sidelock begins to look somewhat naked, like a "spaniel without ears".

Meanwhile, in a remote Scottish Manse, far from the centres of gunmaking a modest Scottish clergyman had been making experiments which were to have far reaching consequences. The story of the Rev. Alexander Forsyth has been told and retold too often to justify repetition here. Forsyth's patent was taken out in 1807 and his guns, which employed loose detonating powder, were built for him by James Purdey after he had left Joseph Manton and prior to Purdey establishing his own business in 1814. In 1809 the Edinburgh gunmaker Innes advertised that he had been appointed sole manufacturer of the Forsyth Patent Gun Lock for Scotland. Innes recommended the new construction with confidence, "the priming is impervious to damp, the inflammation instantaneous, making the aim much more certain and from the complete ignition of the charge, the effect produced in the firing of the gun is increased one third both in Strength and Closeness". The new system, doing away as it did with the tyranny of flint and steel was not immediately acclaimed either by the trade or by sportsmen. As late as 1825 Hawker stated "Can you shoot well with a flint gun? Yes! Then leave well enough alone! Can you? No! Then by all means go and get a detonator!''

The detonator or the percussion shotgun had a relatively brief life but it is of interest, however, and the guns made, and the people who made them, cannot be ignored in any study of the development of the shotgun.

THE DETONATOR

Although the appearance of the detonator solved many of the problems inherent in the flintlock, difficulties which no amount of mechanical ingenuity and skill could surmount, new problems arose. The first of these was how to apply the new principle. In the Forsyth lock loose detonating powder was employed. The Forsyth lock required a high degree of skill in manufacture, by virtue of its construction, to avoid the possibility of igniting not only the priming charge but also the magazine.

One of the earliest alternative systems to achieve any measure of success was the pill or pellet lock. The detonating compound, usually a mixture of potassium chlorate,

A percussion "cap lock" double gun by Forsyth & Co., London. A beautifully made, elegant shotgun with back action lockword dating from c. 1830.

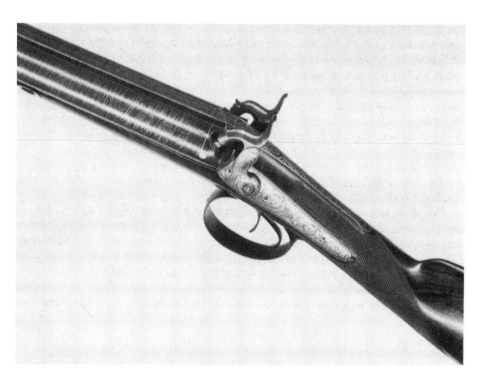

sulphur and charcoal, was mixed with a small amount of gum arabic and made up into a hard pill. Alternatively the compound could be contained between two discs of paper in a manner similar to the present-day toy pistol cap.

Joseph Manton brought out his pellet lock in 1816 (British Patent No. 3985), and in his contemporary advertisement it was claimed "the greatest improvement ever made in guns". This was, to say the least, a gross overstatement. The Manton pellet lock was not a new invention for the use of percussion pellets had been the practice in France and it did not differ in principle from the Forsyth lock. Forsyth was of this opinion and he obtained an injunction to prevent Manton from marketing his "invention" and Forsyth won his case and was awarded nominal damages. The Manton pellet lock had, in addition, practical disadvantages for it was necessary to remove the loose striker from the cock after each shot in order to insert the priming. Undeterred, Joseph Manton took out another patent for gun primers, the percussion tube lock. The pellet lock had not been one of "Old Joe's" successes, but the tube lock worked well and in one of the many variations it proved to be especially favoured by wildfowlers, and continued to be used for muzzle-loading duck- and punt-guns for many years. The restrictions imposed by Forsyth's patent were removed in 1821 when the patent expired. Many ingenious priming devices were invented, some so bizarre that it requires some effort of the imagination to believe that they ever worked.

One such invention was that patented by Baron Heurteloup, a Frenchman living in England, who employed a pewter tube filled from end to end with priming. The hammer was provided with a cutting edge which struck right through the fulminate filled tube. Those familiar with the rather irascible properties of fulminate compounds would expect that the whole tube would have exploded. Heurteloup, however, discovered that by modifying the priming composition it could be cut through with safety and yet detonate when struck by the hammer. Even more improbable was the Sharps disc primer. This was flung into the air from a magazine and caught by the hammer and exploded on the nipple. This system worked quite well except in windy weather!

The most successful system which was to banish into obscurity all other "patent" systems was the humble copper cap. There have been almost as many claimants to the honour of inventing the copper cap as there were nineteenth century gunmakers in Britain. The redoubtable Colonel Hawker himself rather coyly mentions that he had suggested the idea of a copper cap to Joseph Manton, the famous Joseph Egg described himself on his gun case trade labels as the "Inventor of the Percussion Cap," an English artist, Joshua Shaw, resident in Philadelphia, U.S.A., James Purdey and two Frenchmen, Deboubert and Prelat: all have either advanced claims or have had these claims advanced for them. Prelat's addition to his patent of 1818, dated 1820, is the earliest but this does not mean that he was the inventor of the system.

Whoever the inventor was, the copper thimble with the charge of fulminate contained within could be quickly and easily placed upon a hollow nipple com-

Opposite
A "bar action" percussion shotgun by William Greener. A favourite gun
of the author's and one which has been much used.

municating with the powder charge of the gun so that when struck by the hammer it ignited the charge. Low cost, simplicity, and the ability to be used as a conversion for both flint and alternative detonating locks, ensured the success of the copper cap and, it should be remembered, it is still used to this day as the priming for centre-fire cartridges.

In order to get the best results from a percussion gun it was found necessary to adopt a different method of boring the barrels, the practice of constricting the barrel with flint and steel ignition giving rise to excessive recoil when used with percussion ignition. Trouble also arose with the caps. The early type of percussion cap was too brittle and tended to fly to pieces with consequent risk to both the shooter and to those standing nearby. As the system gained adherents, standardisation of cap sizes occurred so that unless some patent type of cap was used, such as the "Patent Imperial Cap" of Samuel & Charles Smith, entirely satisfactory and, of great importance, waterproof, caps were in ready supply in a standard range of sizes to suit most requirements. The minor difficulty of fitting the caps on to the nipples, particularly if the fingers were cold, was overcome by the invention of cap magazines which dispensed the caps as required and which, as the writer can testify from personal experience, worked extremely well.

The most significant feature of percussion muzzle-loading gunmaking was the emergence of the provincial gunmaker. The dominance of London was not eclipsed but it was certainly threatened. Typical of a "best" quality muzzle-loading percussion

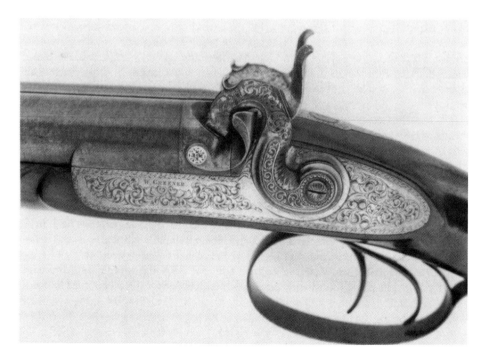

shotgun is the W. Greener illustrated. This is of 17-bore and has 28 in. barrels. Signed, "W. Greener, Maker (By Appointment) to H.R.H. Prince Albert," it is not only a delightful gun to look at but it is also very pleasant to shoot. Greener was only one of several of the new generation of gunsmiths who at one time worked for the Mantons, in Greener's case, John Manton. Greener set up his business in Newcastle before moving to Birmingham. Just as John Manton had resisted the change from flint to percussion, his pupil, Greener, in due time spoke out against the "French Crutch or Breechloading shotgun," stating in 1858 that it was a "specious pretence" and that there was "no possibility of a breechloader ever shooting equal to a well constructed muzzle loader".

THE EARLY BREECHLOADERS

W. Greener's sweeping statement "that no fear need be entertained that the use of breechloaders will become general" must, of course, be taken in the light of contemporary conditions. At the beginning of the second half of the nineteenth century the muzzle-loading percussion shotgun was at the height of its development and, if we disregard the time taken to reload, it was a highly efficient and very handsome firearm. There was still the need to measure out the correct charge of powder for each barrel, but this was easily and quickly done with the powder flask. Also, the danger of the flask exploding was greatly reduced following the introduction of patent flasks with which, even if the worst happened, the sportsman might get no more than a fright when the powder in the measure went off. The need for shot flasks or belts was eliminated with the introduction of Eley's patent cartridges which were to be had in all the common bore sizes as a "packaged unit" with a small wire mesh cage which held the shot together. Admittedly, the powder still had to be poured down the barrel (care being taken not to put two charges in one barrel), and it was still necessary to use the ramrod and also to cap the nipples.

The breechloader, using a cartridge containing the propellent, shot, wad system and means of ignition, was essentially a French development, although the chief architect was a Swiss, Samuel Johannes Pauly. Pauly's most important invention was developed in 1812 in France where he was associated with the gunmaker Prelat. The Pauly system was then improved and adapted by several French gunmakers, Robert and Lefaucheux being the most important. Information on French developments must have been available in Britain but it was not until 1851 that the appearance of the Lefaucheux or, as it was then known, "the French Crutch Gun," at the Great Exhibition at the Crystal Palace brought the first successful breechloading shotgun to the wider attention of the British sporting public. The Lefaucheux gun was fitted with hinged "drop down" barrels and in the absence of contrary information Lefaucheux can be credited with the invention of this system, still widely used today. The chief defect of the system, and one which was quickly pounced upon by the English makers, was the method of bolting the barrels to the action. The breech end of the barrels was provided with a downward projecting piece of metal, the "lump," which passed through a slot cut in the bar of the action body.

On the rear face of the lump a single slot was cut, the "bite". The barrels were bolted by a laterally moving lever which projected along the fore-end, the lever being moved to the right to open the breech. Joseph Lang, who had started in business in 1821 (in 1826 he advertised the entire stock of Joseph Manton), was perhaps the first English maker to introduce the Lefaucheux gun on the British market.

The pinfire cartridge developed by the Frenchman Houillier and patented by him in 1846 had been adopted by Lefaucheux and, although trouble was experienced due to split cases and weak shooting, the pinfire was the first successful shotgun cartridge and enjoyed an amazingly long period of popularity even after the advent of the central-fire cartridge.

The important feature of the pinfire and later true central-fire cartridge was that they had to be extracted from the gun after firing and were reloadable. An alternative was the "needle system," one variation of which was being developed by Dreyse resulting in the formidable Prussian needle gun. In Britain the most successful needle gun was that originally patented by Joseph Needham in 1852 and subsequently

The typical "Lefaucheux" system shotgun: metal fore-end attached to the bar of the action; the barrels secured to the fore-end by a small lever of horn at the fore-end tip; long wooden lever which lies under the fore-end and double bite bolting. This example, a late central-fire double gun, is signed by Dickson of Edinburgh and is not numbered nor recorded.

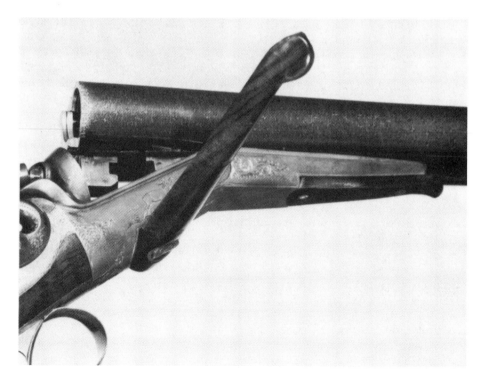

improved by him and by the famous Dublin gunmaker, John Rigby. Needle guns were made by both Needham and Rigby, a Rigby gun marked William & John Rigby, Dublin, No. 10984 being illustrated. This is a beautifully made gun of best quality and it also has the distinction of being the earliest hammerless action to enjoy any measure of popularity. The clean lines of the gun can be seen from the illustration and something of the method of operation from the close-up. Each barrel has its own breech action quite independent of each other. One can be discharged whether the breech of the other is open or closed. To load, the "bolt" handle is lifted upwards, this unlocks the "breech plug" the tapered face of which enters the rear of the barrel. Since

The Needham patent Needle fire gun as made by John Rigby of Dublin. The right-hand "bolt head" has been removed to show the long "needle" from which the system takes its name.

the plug is attached to the rear portion by means of a screw thread the bolt is, in effect, shortened by rotation and unlocked. The whole of the breech plug can then be hinged outwards at right angles to the barrel around the hinge pin, the top of which can be seen projecting from the top of the barrel extension. When the bolt is unlocked the rearward movement of the bolt head also cocks the needle striker, which can be seen protruding from the breech plug. A safety catch which bolts the needle is provided for each lock; when safe the word "Bolted" is disclosed.

With the breech plug open the cartridge is then inserted, the plug is then moved forward about its axis through 90 degrees and the bolt handle pushed downwards

until it engages a small spring catch. The cartridge employed is unusual to modern eyes, since the case lacks an external primer and there is no rim or, indeed, an external metal base. The cap or primer is inside the cartridge and, when struck by the needle (which passes through a hole in the centre of the base of the cartridge), the cap ignites and breaks up and the whole of the cartridge, with the exception of the base wad and internal metal plate which carries the cap, is fired. The base wad is left behind in the breech and is pushed forward when the next cartridge is introduced, to be expelled ahead of the shot when the new cartridge is fired.

Perhaps such a system would be viewed with misgivings if introduced today but this was not the case a century ago. The needle system had some staunch advocates who claimed that, compared with the pinfire system, the needle gun employed cartridges which were half the cost of the pinfire could easily be made by the sportsman himself and which had not to be extracted after firing. One correspondent in 1859 stated that he would be "greatly surprised to find anyone who gave it (the Needham) a fair trial ever using another description of field piece".

The Needham or Rigby needle gun eventually lost ground to the improved pinfire and later central-fire guns. I would very much like to make up some needle gun

Charles Lancaster's patent base-fire double shotgun in original state. The action is partially opened, the barrels having slid forwards before being hinged down.

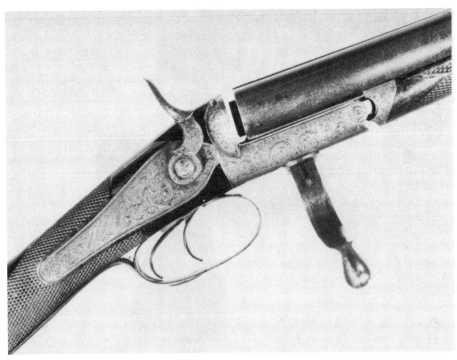

cartridges and try out the system for, as I said, the gun handles extremely well and is beautifully made. It was, however, a blind alley of development and the advances made in both pin and central-fire cartridges and the guns which used them soon rendered the needle gun obsolete.

THE DEVELOPMENT OF THE BREECHLOADER

Improvements in both boring and chambering the pinfire breechloader coupled with the eradiction of faults in the early cartridges resulted in the performance of the breechloader equalling and finally exceeding that of the muzzle loader.

As with flint and steel and the percussion muzzle loader, the pinfire system had its champions, the most vocal being the well known Glasgow gunmaker, James D. Dougall, who, in 1865 stated "that the Lefaucheux or 'pin' cartridge is, for many reasons, the safest and the best". Dougall even went so far as to propose a "better" name for the cartridge, claiming that it was, in effect, a temporary gun-breech and the French term "douille" or socket be employed instead. An advantage claimed for the pinfire was that the cases could be removed from the gun "with the touch of a finger" by means of the protruding pin (other makers of pinfire guns perhaps lacking confidence supplied a small tool for this purpose). Dougall also suggested that "if your cartridges did not fit (perhaps they had been purchased in some foreign or out-of-the-way place) they could be made larger by pasting some thin paper around them, if too large, they should be dried well before the fire and dusted with french chalk".

The first threat to the pinfire came from Charles Lancaster's breechloader. The cartridges were central fire, the base of the cartridge containing a perforated metal disc in the centre of which was the priming. The whole of the base was covered with a metal cap similar to that employed today except, of course, that there was no provision for the percussion cap. The cartridges were more expensive than the pinfire and were not reloadable. Lancaster's cartridges, although representing a step forward, were soon rendered obsolete but his breech action continued to be used with the later type of cartridge.

Lancaster's breech action was far stronger than the original Lefaucheux (and far more expensive) since when the gun was opened the barrels moved forward slightly before hinging downwards. This was accomplished by an underlever which curved backwards over the trigger-guard which, when rotated, moved the barrels forward, withdrawing a projection from a slot cut in the standing breech. When the projection had cleared the slot, the barrels tipped downwards in the normal manner. Lancaster's action was strong and, as befits the barrel maker to Joe Manton, extremely well made. However, when in the open position ready for loading they were somewhat loose, which gave rise to the impression that there was an inherent weakness, unfounded though it was.

Since Lancaster's cartridges had no projecting pin, some means of removing the fired case had to be sought and consequently there appeared the first extractor. Lacking, as one might expect, any extractor, Dougall's patent "Lockfast" breechloader appeared in 1860. Dougall, a "provincial" maker, moved down to London where his breechloader enjoyed success, appearing later as a central-fire gun with extractor when it became obvious that the pinfire was outclassed. The Lockfast system also employed forward moving barrels, and the hinge pin carried an eccentric operated by a lever lying along the bar of the action. The action face or standing breech had disc-shaped projections which, when the barrels were closed, entered recesses at the breech and so ensured positive locking.

The strength and quality of workmanship of the Dougall and the Lancaster are beyond dispute but in ease and speed of handling they were to be eclipsed by yet another invention from France. Patent projection was gained in Britain on 11 June, 1861 in the name of Françoise Eugène Schneider of 13 Rue Gaillon, Paris, for a snap-action central fire gun with an extractor.

The barrels were locked by a round bolt passing through the standing breech into a recess in the barrel lump. The gun is opened by withdrawing the bolt by means of an underlever which then allows the barrels to hinge downwards, in a manner similar to that of the earlier Lefaucheux. The important advantage was that the gun could be closed, and locked, merely by closing the barrels, the snap action bolt locking them securely under spring pressure.

The rights to the Schneider patent were acquired by the London gunmaker, George Henry Daw, who patented improvements on the original Schneider in 1862. The Schneider action was also made in Belgium and will be encountered in a number of variant forms. In Britain the Daw version became very popular due not only to the simple snap action but also to the Daw central fire cartridge which was the direct ancestor of the shotgun cartridge of today.

The Daw was not merely another French invention copied by the British but in a later modification it became, as the Purdey bolt, the most famous of all the barrel locking systems. The round bolt became rectangular in cross-section and instead of a hole the barrel lumps acquired two notches, in the manner of the Lefaucheux, into which the rectangular bolt snugly fitted.

Throughout the whole of the time during which the breechloader was being perfected there was a fascinating interplay of ideas. It is indeed a "tangled skein" since ideas flourished in the rich atmosphere of the Second Empire of France, were often translated into wood and metal in the workshops of Liège and then sold under the names of British gunmakers in the U.K. French ideas were brought into Britain, altered and modified and then sold by the great names of the London and provincial trade.

Due consideration must be given to the contribution made to the development of the breech loading shotgun by the French but the efforts of the British gun trade were by no means restricted to improving and modifying ideas imported from across the Channel.

One of the most widely used actions of all time, the "double grip screw underlever" was, according to the famous W. W. Greener, "the invention of a Birmingham gunmaker" and "is substantially the same as the original Lefaucheux". These statements, which are repeated throughout the editions of Greener's book, *The Gun and its Development*, were accepted and subsequently repeated.

Much of the history associated with the development of the shotgun is obscure, confused, distorted and often, quite simply, just forgotten! Aided and abetted by the traditional secrecy of the gun trade and further fuelled by rivalry and jealousy it often amazes me that so much of the history has been preserved. More often than not this is due to the manner in which the guns of the period were made rather than to paper records which were either not kept or subsequently destroyed.

A search through the patent records brings to light the name of the Birmingham gunmaker whose neglect by both Greener and Walsh has denied him the recognition which he undoubtedly merited. His name was H. Jones, the date of his patent 1859. From the patent drawing the details become apparent. The barrel lump has a slot cut through it effectively making it into two lumps, the front, which hinges over the pin and about which the barrels rotate and the rear lump which has a further slot or "bite" cut into the front face to match a similar slot in the rear face of the front lump.

The patent describes how the barrels are locked "by pieces on the boss of a transversely-moving locking lever". It is perhaps better to regard the mechanism as an interrupted screw thread operated by a rotating underlever which when closed passes over the bow of the trigger guard. It can also be regarded, as stated by Greener, as a modification of the Lefaucheux action by the provision of a second lump and bite or grip and the reversal of the locking lever, which, it will be remembered, lay along the fore-end of the original Lefaucheux. The situation is further complicated by the appearance in France of a double grip Lefaucheux action which is sometimes referred to as the "fermeture à T, système Lefaucheux" and a similar system but with the rear facing lever of the Jones action known as the "Fermeture à T, système Beringer". The Beringer gun does not appear to have been patented in Britain and its chief claim to fame is the unusual cartridge it employed. It was, in effect, a rim fire case fired by a captive firing pin mounted on top of the barrel and could, therefore, be almost mistaken for a loaded pinfire gun. A single bite and downward hinged barrels reflected the influence of Lefaucheux but the underlever formed the trigger guard and was, of course, rearward facing like the Jones which was to appear some ten years later.

It is at this point one cannot help but wonder if Henry Jones had encountered one of the Beringer shotguns and if this had led him to the use of the rear-facing lever. The Jones action is important for a number of reasons and will be dealt with in greater detail later in the book.

A number of other double grip screw actions appeared and various modifications and improvements were offered to culminate in a patent by Alex Henry of Edinburgh for a screw double grip action hammerless gun where the rotary underlever not only unlocked the barrels but also cocked the firing mechanism.

Fortunately for those who wished to make the new breechloader, lockwork suitable had already appeared – on the back-action lock. In this type of lock the mainspring is carried on the lockplate to the rear of the tumbler instead of in front. Later it was found possible to cut away the bar of the action to accommodate the mainspring of a "bar" action lock as it then became known, but since many thought that the bar of the action was weakened unnecessarily, bar action side-plates were employed with back-action lockwork. The bar of the lockplate being inletted into the metal of the action body did tend to strengthen the action since the rest of the lockplate supported the inletted portion of the stock. An important innovation was the introduction of rebounding locks. The gunmaker had adapted and altered the lockwork and furniture of the muzzle loader, new components had been introduced and before long the criterion "that it (the breechloader) did not look very different from a muzzle loader" no longer held. Instead of relying on Continental ideas, the British gunmaker was to introduce his own, and before the century was out the Patent Office was deluged with patents, some of which were of fundamental importance and merit our later consideration.

SUCCESSES AND FAILURES

A quick glance at the contemporary scene during the mid-1860s gives the impression that the breechloader was supreme. It certainly was in France but if we take a look at the guns on the line at the July Pigeon Shooting Handicap in 1864 we find that twenty-four competitors still used muzzle loaders against twenty-seven using breechloaders and that Purdey guns were preferred, either in breech or muzzle-loading style, to all others. No mention is made as to whether the breechloaders were pin or central fire but the ordinary sporting man was apt to complain that, whilst the Lancaster or Daw were

The most famous of all mid-nineteenth century snap actions. The Purdey "Thumb-Hole" of 1863. This uses the second type of lever which, with the spring, can be seen attached to the trigger plate. The flat Purdey bolt slides in the bar of the action; this is a "bar-in-the-wood" gun.

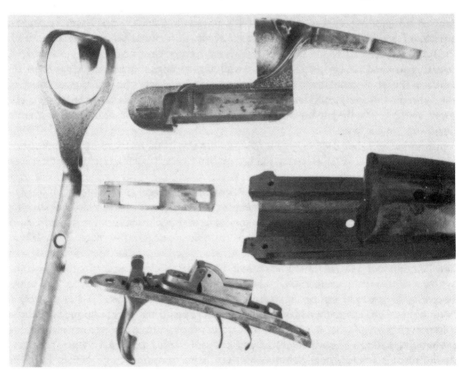

the best breechloaders, "there was some difficulty in obtaining cartridges". Patents had been taken out for methods of converting muzzle loaders to breech-loaders, Thomas Sylven of the Strand specialising in such work. For the owners of a breechloader who could not get a supply of his central fire cartridges, several types of "patent" converter were obtainable to perform the reverse service, from breechloader to muzzle loader.

As previously mentioned, one feature of this period was the emergence of the provincial maker. The use of trade advertising, a widely distributed sporting Press and better means of communication, were all factors which helped the country gunmaker plus, of course, the significant advantages of lower prices.

Apart from the Birmingham makers who no doubt thought that they should get a slice of the cake, Greener, father and son, Needham, Smith, Elliot, Harlow and others, we find J. Erskine of Newton Stewart, "North Britain"; Snowie, Inverness; Fletcher, Gloucester; T. Turner, Reading; Jefferies, Norwich; Thos. Newton, Manchester; Edinburgh makers, Dickson, Alex. Thomson, Mortimer, MacLauchlan and others.

A number of the provincial makers were to capitalise on their popularity by moving their business to London; others established shops so that their guns could bear the London address, a cachet of importance. Dougall of Glasgow, without doubt one of the most vocal of all gunmakers and a pioneer of Press publicity, was to establish himself in London; Pape of Newcastle preferred to stay where he was but he put out the first illustrated advertisment followed closely by W. W. Greener, of St. Mary's Works, Birmingham, who was at pains to point out that he had "no business connection with my father", old William himself being a champion to the last of the muzzle loader and doubtless dismissing his son's new breechloader with contempt.

To aid the user of the new breechloader, and help reduce the cost of cartridges, reloading was practised, Jefferies of Norwich inventing the first of such loading tools for the pinfire cartridge, being followed by Morrison, also of Norwich, Hawkesley of Sheffield and Melland. Besides Eley's cartridges could be obtained from continental sources and at first they were of superior quality. Later, Eley's had competition from Bussey of London and E. & A. Ludlow of Legge Street, Birmingham, and in 1866 the centuries-long dominance of blackpowder was first threatened by "guncotton", Messrs. Prentice & Co., of Stowmarket offering cartridges on a commercial scale loaded with smokeless powder.

What of the guns during this embryonic stage of the breechloader? For the next half century the gunmakers had an unparalleled market for their wares. Britain was at the height of her power, a select but growing number of people had a purchasing capacity unrivalled anywhere else in the world and the gunmakers eagerly competed for a share in this wealth, offering a bewildering number of patent actions, improvements and new designs to tempt the well-to-do sportsman.

The aim was to produce a gun which harmoniously combined the following desirable attributes. Ease and simplicity of manipulation, the gun had to open and close without undue effort and reloading had to be quick and easy. Ample strength, a criticism of the Lefaucheux type of action was lack of strength – a person accustomed to the rigidity of the muzzle loader needed to be convinced that a gun which "broke in the middle" was not liable to do so on firing!

Those used to the classic lines of the muzzle loader would not tolerate for long, undue bulk, lumps and bits and pieces sticking out at all angles which, apart from aesthetic considerations, could cause bumps and bruises when the gun was fired or even just carried. Last of all was the continual striving for lightness. Even the grand Victorian might feel aggrieved if at the end of a day's hard shooting he felt the need of a gun carriage to transport his newly acquired, but rather heavy, breechloader back to his gunroom. The Lancaster, for example, tipped the scales at over 8 lb.

By 1870 there were so many "patent" actions that a simple chronological listing is inadequate. However, they can be classified by the method employed to attach the barrels and the means used to bolt the barrels. First of all there was the Lefaucheux with the operating lever along the fore-end, originally with a single grip or bite and later with the double grip. The modified Lefaucheux with the lever to the rear curved around the trigger guard, again, originally with a single bite and then modified to a double grip or bite and as such, a classic type of breech action. With the rotary bolt there were several modifications, such as the Lang, where the bolt was operated by a top-lever instead of an underlever. Then Schneider and Daw's patents for a bolt passing through the standing breech into the lump. There were modifications of this system, the most important being that of Purdey who introduced the flat bolt locking into two bites in the lumps, the most widely employed method of locking yet devised.

The alternative was to combine the drop-down barrel with a forward movement. The Lancaster and Dougall "Lockfast" were on this plan and proved to be extremely strong and robust. In both of these systems the barrels moved forward but a short distance to unlock. In the Bastin, patented in 1860, the barrels slide forward along the fore-end and were locked by a lever which lay under the fore-end. Guns of this type were made by Cogswell of London but like the Jefferies first patented in 1862 in which the barrels were hinged to move laterally defects were found and both types of mechanism fell into disuse. The simple hinged drop-down barrel locked by a Purdey bolt operated by the top-lever eventually became the standard breech mechanism to which was added in the central fire gun an extractor system. To simplify the operation of the gun, self-cocking actions were to be developed and these led on to the "hammerless actions".

THE BREECHLOADER PERFECTED

If we pause for a moment to consider the objectives of the gunmaker the most important consideration was the ease and speed of loading. For example, due to the "overhang" of the pinfire hammer it was necessary to half cock the hammers before the breech could be opened. This meant an extra operation and for a time "self-half-cocking" pinfires became the vogue. The hammers could be half cocked by the lever which opened the breech, W. W. Greener introducing such an action in 1864. Of greater importance was the invention of the rebounding hammer patented by Stanton in 1869 which, when employed with spring retracting firing pins, did much to eliminate the hazard of accidental discharge when the breech was closed. The protrusion of firing pins or strikers did cause several serious accidents prompting W. W. Greener to

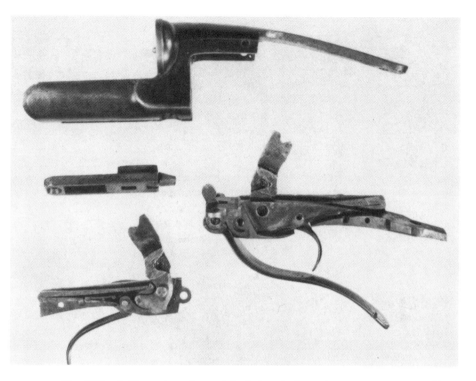

The Gibbs & Pitt action of 1879. The bolt, which can be seen under the action bar, is pulled to the rear by the long operating lever. As it moves to the rear to free the barrel, the hinged, wedge-shaped rear enters the recess in the hammers and cocks them. The greatly modified back action locks are attached to the trigger plate.

introduce his retractable strikers which were pulled back by a small catch on the breast of the hammer, and in 1868 Horseley made strikers which were retracted by a camming surface on the breast of the hammer engaging a lever. Horseley also incorporated an indicator which disclosed the word "Loaded" when there was a cartridge in the chamber.

The sixties also saw the introduction of Westley Richards' "doll's head" top rib extension originally employed as the sole bolting, to be quickly followed by Greener's cross bolt which was later to be combined with the Purdey bolt producing the famous Greener "Treble Wedge-Fast" action. Once the protection provided by patent expired, the Purdey bolt became widely used, and the numerous single snap bolts, with the exception of William Powell's single bolt, became obsolete. Powell's bolt was operated by a top-lever which, instead of being pushed laterally to the right, was lifted. Although perhaps not as convenient as the conventional top-lever the Powell system enjoyed a measure of success.

In the seventies attention was directed towards the elimination of the need to cock

An alternative method of cocking "hammerless" guns was that employed by Tolley of Birmingham. The top lever retracts the Purdey type bolt seen under the bar of the action and as the barrels open an extension pushes back the two action bars, one still attached to the cocking piece, the other in place in the bar of the action. These action bars, or limbs, push against the breast of the internal hammers, cocking them as the barrels fall.

the hammers manually. Several systems appeared but the importance of work on self-cocking hammer guns was the fact that this work prepared the way for the self-cocking hammerless action. If we discount the "hammerless" needle guns such as the Needham, the earliest self-cocking guns to achieve any measure of popularity were those in which the lever which unbolted the barrels was used to cock the hammers. T. Murcott's hammerless gun of 1871 employed an extension to the underlever which drew back the bolt and also cocked the internal tumblers of the lock to which were attached the strikers. Gibbs and Pitt of Bristol perfected their hammerless self-cocking gun in 1879. This action employed lever-cocking but utilised the bolt itself, an extension to which entered recesses formed in the internal hammers so that when the bolt was retracted by the underlever, the hinged extension to the bolt cocked the hammers. A very interesting feature of the Gibbs gun is the manner in which the lockwork has been modified and is contained within a "case" which projects from beneath the gun. Allport and Henry both modified the "double grip" underlever action so that the action of opening the gun once again cocked the hammers. I was fortunate to be able to buy an Alex. Henry gun working on this principle which had originally been made as a 0.577 double rifle and subsequently converted to a 3 in. 12-bore. For this reason it was still very sound and I have used the gun for wildfowling for several years and although the underlever is slower than the toplever, the extra effort needed to cock the action is not noticeable.

The first hammerless gun employing the fall of the barrels to cock the action was invented by W. Anson and J. Deeley. The action itself represented the first radical development rather than a modification of existing mechanisms and for this reason the A & D action will be dealt with later. To illustrate how the mechanism of a sidelock gun was altered to permit cocking by the fall of the barrel, Henry Tolley's gun of 1886 can be used. It will be noticed that as the cocking bars occupy the space in the action bar normally filled by the lock mainspring, the Tolley locks are back actioned with a sham bar lock-plate.

The 1870s were notable not only for the many self-cocking actions which appeared, but also for the energy devoted to the provision of safety devices, the need for which became increasingly apparent with the development of hammerless actions. Yet another preoccupation of the gunmaker of this period was the need to provide some means of showing whether or not the gun was cocked. Once the external hammers had been removed there was no indication of whether or not the action was cocked. Some makers provided cocking indicators which protruded from the top of the action body to show that the hammers inside were cocked, others like Scott provided little round windows in the lockplates so that the position of the internal hammers could be verified by visual inspection.

In 1879 James MacNaughton of Edinburgh introduced his "Trigger Plate" action which was originally cocked by the toplever. A typical MacNaughton action is the "Edinburgh" action where the metal of the action body is cut away to permit the wood of the stock to be carried forward. In this there is a similarity to the earlier Purdey action but the long top strap and massive trigger plate strengthen the hand of the stock, a noticeable weakness in earlier "skeleton" stocks. T. W. Webley introduced a "trigger plate" action in the following year and in 1883 Dickson and Murray patented

The MacNaughton "Trigger Plate" action with lever cocking. The internal hammers are cocked by an extension to the flat locking bolt in a manner similar to the Gibbs & Pitt. The long top lever is required to aid cocking; later the action was modified for barrel cocking.

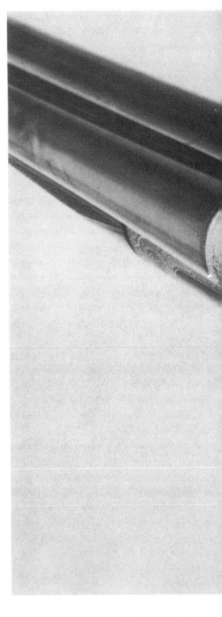

their three-barrelled gun, based also on a trigger-plate action, a modification of which was to be the famous Dickson "Round Action", a type of mechanism which is fortunately still being built. The Dickson three-barrelled gun appeared shortly after Lancaster's four-barrelled gun patented by H. A. A. Thorn in 1881.

The eighties saw many unusual inventions besides the multi-barrelled guns which

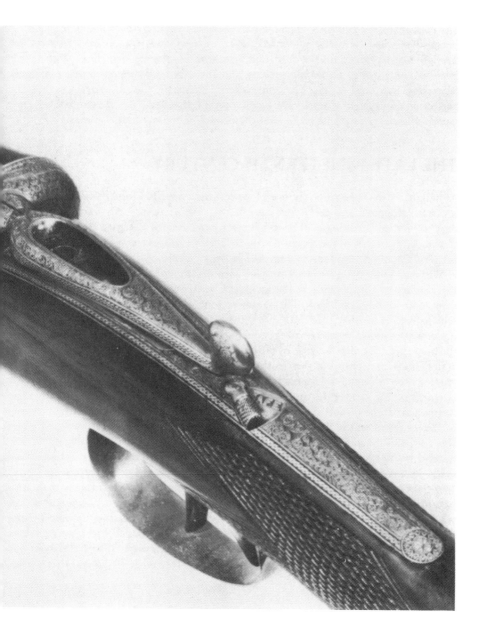

enjoyed a brief vogue. One of these was Henri Pieper's electric shotgun, Bentley
introduced a self-cocking gun with hammers inlet into the outside of the lockplate, the
hammers lacking a comb and serving as indicators, and Scott appreciating the extra
effort required to open or close the gun when cocking was performed by this operation
introduced his solution, which was to cock one hammer when the barrels were opened

and cock the other hammer when the barrels were closed. Barrel cocking in one form or another was eventually to replace lever cocking since for obvious reasons full strength mainsprings could be used, and there was less chance of misfires. With simple opening and closing, automatic cocking and automatic safeties one chore remained, extracting the fired cases. The gunmakers' attention was diverted towards the perfection of a system whereby the cases could be expelled from the gun entirely, not merely withdrawn sufficiently so that they could be removed by the fingers.

THE LATE NINETEENTH CENTURY

Although, as we have seen, the breechloader originated in France, those responsible for its development and perfection were British. Verification of this is simple. One has only to pick up a catalogue of breechloading guns, French, German, Italian, Spanish, Czech, Russian to find the terms, Anson & Deeley action, Greener Cross Bolt, Purdey action, Holland & Holland system and so on.

Without doubt the most revolutionary idea was that of Anson & Deeley. First of all the number of components in the lockwork were greatly reduced. There were only three main limbs in each lock. The hammer, tumbler or striker is provided with an arm which projects forward into the bar of the action. The mainspring acts on this arm and underneath the end is one arm of the cocking lever which is pivoted concentrically with the hinge pin. The shorter limb of the cocking lever protrudes through the joint of the action body and enters a slot in the fore-end. When the barrels are dropped for loading, the fore-end is depressed, thus rotating the cocking lever which pushes upwards on the arm of the tumbler until the tumbler is held at full cock by the third component of the system, the sear. As originally made by Westley Richards, the Anson & Deeley relied on the Westley Richards doll's head extension. Later the Purdey bolt was added to the locking system and modifications were made to the original action, notably by W. W. Greener. Most countries with an indigenous arms industry have made Anson & Deeley type guns in one form or another. The rather square "box" shape has been modified over the years and also one finds A & D actions with dummy side-plates, so that to the uninitiated the gun presents the external appearance of a sidelock. Many makers made a speciality of the A & D type of action, notably Westley Richards, who were later to introduce their "hand detachable" locks, and Greener with his many variations and "improvements". In Edinburgh, Joseph Harkom was famous for his A & D guns which were justifiably acclaimed. The A & D action was

Top right

A 20 bore example of the Wesley Richards A & D action. This early gun is locked solely by means of the "doll's head" extension and is still in use today.

Bottom right

A contemporary advert for the Westley Richards.

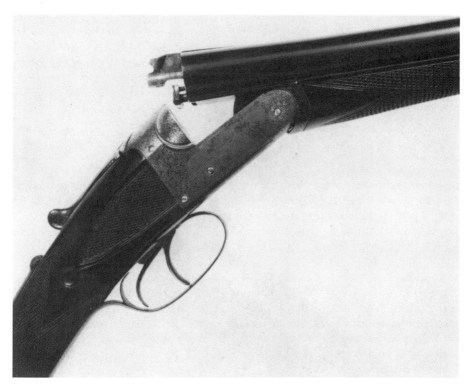

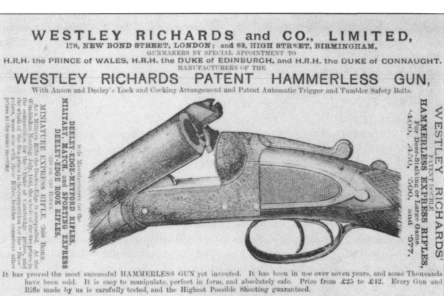

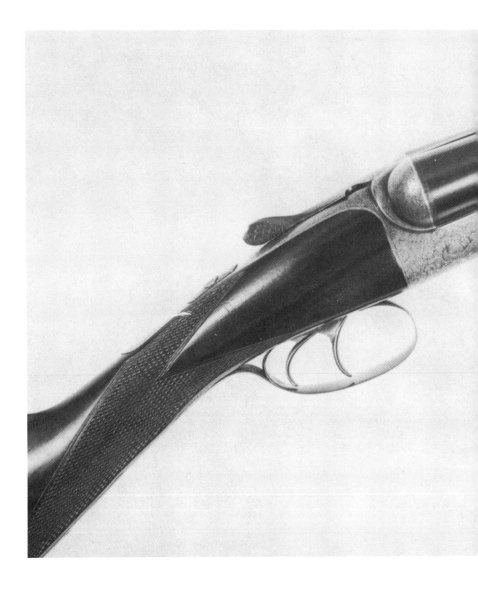

further improved in 1886 by J. Deeley, who added his ejector mechanism. Ejectors had been fitted to guns for some time, the earliest being J. Needham's self-cocking ejector gun of 1874.

When you think about it, the selective ejector mechanism is quite ingenious. It has several functions to perform. First the mechanism must withdraw unfired cases from the breech sufficiently for them to be removed by hand. Second, the mechanism has to select which cartridge has been fired and only eject the fired cases. Third, its incorporation must not increase the weight, bulk or difficulty of operating the gun.

The Dickson "Round Action" gun. This example was one of four made in 1911, and is one of the most graceful hammerless shotguns ever built.

This includes not only the work involved in operating the ejector springs but also dismantling and reassembling the gun.

Ejector mechanisms can be roughly divided into two types, those in which the mechanism is in the action body of the gun and those where the mechanism is separate from the lockwork, usually in the fore-end.

The Dickson Round Action is an example, still being made, of the ejector mechanism being housed in the action body of the gun. Since this is a "special" action, the ejector mechanism is unique and has not been employed by anyone else. Deeley's ejector is housed in the fore-end with the exception of the "trigger" which is in the knuckle of the action body. In the Dickson ejector the springs are compressed by two levers which protrude from the table of the action bar, in Deeley's ejector the springs are compressed by the extractor when the gun is closed. During the eighties and nineties well over twenty patents were taken out by gunmakers for ejector systems. Apart from special mechanisms, such as the Dickson, two types have enjoyed widespread adoption, the Deeley and the Southgate.

During the nineties considerable effort was also devoted to the perfection of single-trigger mechanisms for double guns. The idea of discharging two barrels successively with one trigger was not new but, as far as I know, selective single-trigger mechanisms were a late nineteenth century development.

I must leave until later a more detailed treatment of single-trigger mechanisms, but the great number which were developed can be classified simply into "Three pull systems", "Delay systems" and "Pendulum" or inertia systems.

Even a cursory browse through the dense jungle of the single-trigger patents would make it very apparent that all possible systems have been considered long ago. However, as recently as 1962 a new idea was patented by Fausto Massi, gunmaker of Vicenza in Northern Italy. One of the advantages of a double gun is the ability to select the right degree of choke or pattern for the type of game or the range. This is possible, since traditionally the degree of choke in each barrel differs. With a non-selective single-trigger mechanism the right barrel is fired first. With a selective single-trigger mechanism time has to be spent on moving the selector if the left barrel is to be fired first. In the Fausto Massi system the gun is fitted with two triggers, the front being capable of firing both the right and left hand barrels as a single trigger. The rear trigger fires the left, or second, barrel only. The single trigger works on the inertia principle and the mechanism can be adopted to most double guns.

It can, of course, be argued that it takes no longer to set the selector mechanism as it does to move the finger from the front to the rear trigger if one wishes to fire the left barrel first. However, it is an interesting idea and serves, if nothing else, to show that there are still ingenious men capable of fresh thought and new ideas when one might have expected that all possible avenues of attack had been thoroughly explored.

NEW IDEAS

Ingenuity was displayed in abundance at the turn of the century for two new ideas were to appear and challenge the supremacy of the side-by-side double breechloader. The first was to place the barrels on top of each other, instead of side-by-side, the second to introduce magazine or repeating shotguns.

As with so many "new" inventions, the vertical rather than the horizontal arrangement of the barrels was of considerable antiquity. This style had been popular on the continent for wheel-lock, flint and percussion weapons but since the manufacture of breechloaders presented several different problems, the over-and-under breechloading shotgun was a comparative latecomer. In Britain some of the initial attempts to build guns on this pattern were not particularly happy. The use of the standard downward projecting barrel lumps and conventional locking produced guns of inordinate depth, lacking in those desirable attributes of grace and line which had been an enviable heritage of British skill and craftmanship.

Two over-and-under guns surmounted this difficulty, the first was the Boss, the original patents for which had been obtained in 1909, and the second, the Woodward. In both cases the bottom lumps are discarded and locking is achieved by bites located towards the centre of the barrel group. The "lumps" are situated on each side of the lower barrel and this system has produced over-and-under guns having little, if any, increased depth compared with the side-by-side double. Without doubt one of the best known over-and-under shotguns is the Browning, the last brain child of John M. Browning and a remarkable feat of engineering. Manufacture of the Browning was just starting at the time of the inventor's death in 1926.

There is one bite under the lower barrel but the action depth is not noticeably gross. An unusual feature is that the fore-end is not detachable, remaining attached to the barrels when the gun is taken down. Still in production by Fabrique Nationale d'Armes de Guerre, s.a., of Herstal, near Liège, the Browning is offered in a variety of finishes and with ventilated rib, single trigger and automatic safety. Like many British shotgun designs it is now widely copied. The Browning was not made in America and, indeed, the manufacture of high quality shotguns in the land of mass production has always presented problems which have never been satisfactorily overcome. Certain makers enjoyed a well-deserved reputation, amongst them being Parker Bros. who made their first shotgun in 1868. The original design was discarded in favour of basic

The Boss "Over and Under" gun considered by many to be the best of
the British O/Us. This example is fitted with a single trigger and is
marked Boss's Patent 1909.

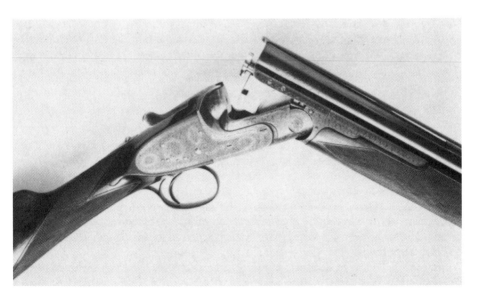

John Browning's O/U designed in America and manufactured by Fabrique Nationale in Liège, Belgium. Commercially, it is the most successful of all the O/U designs and the most widely copied.

Deeley features in 1879 and a hammerless action was adopted in 1889. In 1934 the company was bought by Remington and the manufacture of shotguns was not resumed after the Second World War.

Unusual in American domestic manufactured shotguns, the L. C. Smith employed side-locks, the first being made about 1889. Made by the Hunter Arms Co. Inc. of

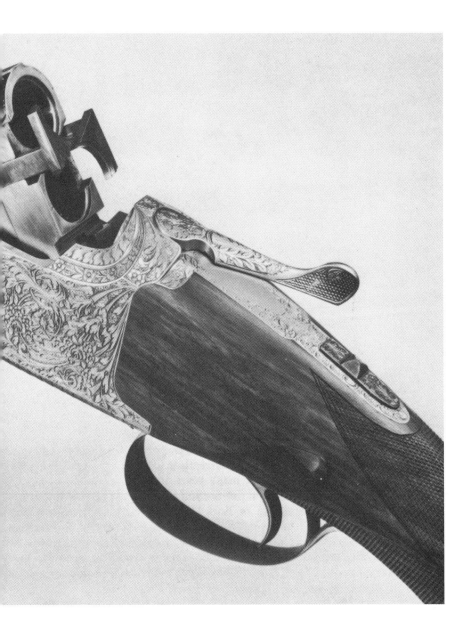

Fulton, N.Y., the L. C. Smith double barrel guns were made in a wide range of grades based on the same design. Manufacture ceased in 1950.

In the over-and-under designs that of Remington possibly enjoyed the greatest success. The Model 32 used top bolting, the top of the breech sliding back and forth, in the closed position covering the top of the upper barrel. High costs resulted in this gun

Recent research has shown that Germany may well be the home of the modern O/U. This example of a type currently in production employs the Kersten bolt to lock the barrels. By Simpson of Suhl this is one of the lower priced options available.

being discontinued but a similar locking system is employed by Valmet Oy of Finland for their over-and-under "Lion" shotgun, currently in production. Due to low cost the Marlin over-and-under sold well for many years and the Savage over-and-under rifle/shotgun 0.22 rf or 0.22 Magnum rim-fire and 0.410 shot is a useful little gun.

In Germany the over-and-under or Bock-Doppelflinte has long been popular. Available from a number of makers with sidelocks, Anson and Deeley, or Blitz trigger plate actions, the locking systems employed are traditionally Kersten top cross-bolt with standard double bite under bolting. The Kersten cross-bolt is similar to the Greener except that twin-barrel lugs are employed. When under bolting is used this leads to the usual problems of excessive depth in the action body.

The more unusual German breech actions such as the Stendenbach and the Schuler no longer appear to be made and it is Italy where we find the oldest firearm factory in the world, Pietro Beretta, manufacturing an unusual shotgun which is bolted by two cylindrical bolts from the breech face which enter locking recesses positioned at either side of the upper barrel. No other bolting is provided and the locking is secure since the locking recesses are machined out of the solid breeching, the well-known Beretta "Monobloc". This type of bolting is used for the Series "S" over-and-under shotguns, the Series "SO" being fitted with sidelocks and bolted by double extensions from the top barrel and a cross-bolt. Similar bolting is used on over-and-under shotguns made by Piotti of Gardone, and on the Model "Delfino" made by Antonio Zoli of Gardone.

The Franchi Model 63 employs Browning-type bolting as does the Breda "Sirio". The Czechoslovak ZH series of over-and-under shotguns adopt a top sliding breech coupled with Kersten-type cross-bolt but their most interesting feature is the availability of a series of interchangeable barrels and interchangeable stocks. The over-and-under barrel arrangement has also had its fair share of unusual breech closures, the "Victor" made by Fabbrica Nazionale Armi of Brescia being one example. In this design, the barrels slid forward supported by two cylindrical rods and in the French "G. Bretton" wide use was made of light alloy, the barrels were fixed and the breech block slid to the rear. The design is somewhat similar to the more widely known side-by-side double shotgun, the French Darne, which can trace its ancestry back to the patents of Charlin and Santiot in 1904, and then almost to the beginning of breechloaders since the Pauly, and the later Robert, employed fixed barrels and a movable breech.

Although a side-by-side "double" the American Ostrander four-shot repeating shotgun serves to end this phase of shotgun development and to introduce the next, the repeating shotgun. The Ostrander, which I first encountered in the British patents of 1894, is one of those guns which must be seen to be believed. After examining the patent drawings I considered it unlikely that one was ever built. However, one thing I have learned, anything is possible where firearms are concerned and to my surprise I later found that the four-shot twin-barrelled magazine gun was, in fact, manufactured by Ostrander Repeating Gun Co. of East Boston, Mass., and apparently not only were they produced, but the existence of at least one example indicates that people perhaps even bought them!

REPEATING SHOTGUNS

Repeating shotguns have been made employing most of the available systems, revolving, bolt-action, slide-action, lever-action and so on. One of the earliest repeating shotguns to achieve any measure of commercial success was the Spencer. Christopher Spencer was a typical figure of the late nineteenth century American industrial scene. He took out patents for textile machinery and later designed a seven shot repeating rifle which saw wide use during the American Civil War. In 1882 he organised a firm to manufacture the repeating shotgun which bears his name but the venture failed and he concentrated on machine tool design, a field in which he prospered. The Spencer employed a tubular magazine under the barrel and it was operated by a sliding "hand piece" or movable fore-end and, as such, was the father of the many slide, pump or "trombone" action shotguns which followed.

One of the many alternative methods of operation which were proposed was that

Overleaf
A beautifully restored example of Spencer's Model 1882 slide action
shotgun.

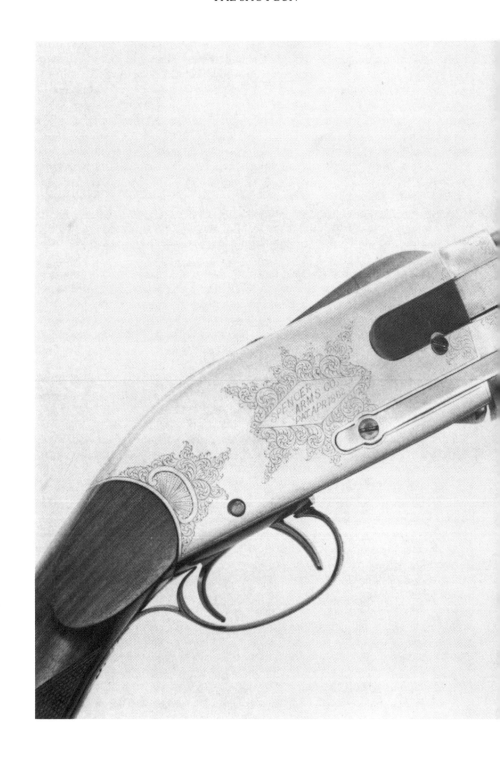

Winchester's highly successful slide or pump action Model of 1897,
countless numbers of which are still in use. Plain and "Fancy" versions
of this model are shown in the catalogue.

used by the Burgess. The Burgess Gun Company of Buffalo, N.Y., was active for but a
brief period, 1892–9, and the principal product was the unique sliding pistol grip
which moved to the rear for extraction and ejection. The Burgess had top ejection and
an external hammer.

In 1887 Winchester introduced the first shotgun made by themselves, the lever-
action Model of 1887; this model continued in production until 1901 when it was
redesigned as the Model 1901 and finally dropped from the selling range in 1920. With
the exception of bolt-action shotguns which have always enjoyed limited success
because of their low price, the slide action is without doubt the basic type of repeating
mechanism. In 1890 Winchester purchased a patent from the Browning Bros. of
Ogden, Utah, for a slide-action gun which was manufactured and sold as the
Winchester Model 1893. It was not successful and an improved version, the 1897
Model, was then introduced. This gun, with its external hammer, was one of the most
successful repeating shotguns ever made; its manufacture continued until 1957.
Enjoying equal popularity the Winchester Model 12 was developed by Thomas C.
Johnson and introduced in 1912. By 1943 one million had been made and it is still in
limited production, being partially superseded by the Winchester Model 1200.

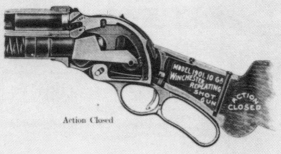

Winchester Repeating Arms Co. *WINCHESTER* New Haven, Connecticut, U.S.A.

GUNS AND AMMUNITION

Winchester Lever Action Repeating Shotgun
Model 01

Action Closed

To dismount the gun, take out the mainspring with the aid of a pair of pliers. Compress the mainspring, and draw it backwards through the hammer slot in the breech block. Remove the right and left carrier screws. Lift the carrier out through the top of the gun. Push out the breech block pin, and remove breech block and hammer. To take out the extractor, push the extractor against the lower side of its slot. Push back the extractor spring pin with the point of a knife, and push the extractor hook towards the breech block stud. The firing pin is removed by taking out the firing pin stop pin. To remove the trigger, unscrew the trigger spring screw. Drive out the trigger pin.

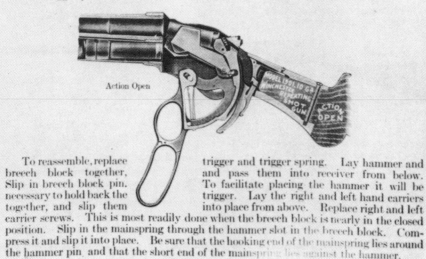

Action Open

To reassemble, replace breech block together, Slip in breech block pin. necessary to hold back the together, and slip them carrier screws. This is most readily done when the breech block is nearly in the closed position. Slip in the mainspring through the hammer slot in the breech block. Compress it and slip it into place. Be sure that the hooking end of the mainspring lies around the hammer pin and that the short end of the mainspring lies against the hammer.

trigger and trigger spring. Lay hammer and and pass them into receiver from below. To facilitate placing the hammer it will be trigger. Lay the right and left hand carriers into place from above. Replace right and left

Winchester's second attempt at a lever action shotgun, the Model of 1901. Unlike the lever action rifles, the shotguns made on this system were ungainly, cumbersome weapons.

Winchester Repeating Arms Co. *WINCHESTER* New Haven, Connecticut, U.S.A.

GUNS AND AMMUNITION

Winchester Hammerless Repeating Shotgun
Model 12

Standard 12 Gauge, Model 12, 6 Shots

Thirty-inch nickel steel barrel, pistol grip stock and action slide handle of plain walnut, not checked, rubber butt plate.

Standard 16 or 20 Gauge, Model 12, 6 Shots

16 Gauge
Twenty-six inch nickel steel barrel, pistol grip stock and action slide handle of plain walnut, not checked, rubber butt plate.

20 Gauge
Twenty-five inch nickel steel barrel, pistol grip stock and action slide handle of plain walnut, not checked, rubber butt plate.
Shorter or longer barrels not furnished on either 16 or 20 gauge guns.

Tournament Gun, 12 Gauge only, Model 12, 6 Shots

Thirty-inch full choke nickel steel barrel, with raised matted rib. Handsome stock of selected walnut, oil finished, with well-shaped straight grip, checked; rubber butt plate. Action slide handle of selected walnut, checked. The length of pull is 14 inches, drop at comb 1½ inches, and drop at heel 1⅞ inches. These dimensions have been worked out with a great deal of thought and care, to make the gun fit the average trap shooter's requirements and, therefore, handle well. The comb is heavy and rounding, which is a help to quick and accurate shooting, and also minimizes cross-sighting. The Tournament grade gun will be made according to the above specifications, the only exceptions being length of stock and bore of barrels. Stocks not more than one inch shorter than the standard, and with not more than one inch extra drop at heel, will be furnished at an additional cost. Barrels with cylinder bore or modified choke will be furnished without extra charge, if so specified.

Winchester's Model 12 slide action shotgun, three versions of which are illustrated in a catalogue dating from before World War II. It is one of the classic all-time greats of slide action shotgun design.

Remington were slightly later in the repeating shotgun stakes. They, of course, had a range of good quality double shotguns on the market, the first of which appeared in 1873. In 1907 they introduced their Model 10 hammerless, slide-action repeating shotgun which was manufactured under Pedersen patents. This was followed by the Model 17, of similar design but made in 20-bore only. The Model 29, introduced in 1929, replaced the Model 10. All of these guns featured bottom ejection and the Ithaca Model 37 is today's representative of this type of action. Remington then produced their Model 31 with a side ejection port similar to the Model 12 Winchester which was kept on the range until 1949, when it was displaced by the model 870 "Wingmaster", Remington's current slide-action shotgun.

As with the slide-action, the self-loading or "automatic" shotgun was primarily an American invention. The Remington Model 11 autoloader was based on John M. Browning's patents of 1900. The design had originally been offered to Winchester but Browning and Winchester disagreed on terms and the design was made as the Model 11 by Remington and introduced in 1905 in 12-, 16- and 20-bore and in several quality grades. Two years before, in 1903, Fabrique Nationale manufactured the Browning design under licence and as the Browning Automatic Shotgun it is still in production. This 1900 vintage design has been more widely copied than any other; for example, the Breda and Franchi autoloading shotguns are of basic Browning design as are many other American and European automatic shotguns. Remington dropped the Model 11 in 1948 with the introduction of Model 11–48 which was eventually made in 12, 16, 20, 28 and 0.410 calibres, and is still on the selling range.

The first successful basic design change took place in 1954, when Winchester brought out their Model 50 autoloader. The traditional auto-shotgun is the long recoil type where the barrel slides back and forth; the barrel and breech, locked together, recoil about three inches, the breech is unlocked and latched in the rear position, the barrel moves forward, unlatches the breech which then moves under the drive of its recoil spring, chambering the new cartridge before locking itself to the barrel. The man responsible for the idea behind the Model 50 was David "Carbine" Williams with his movable breech chamber. The Model 50 operates on the "short" recoil principle, and the later Model 59 added something new again, the steel and glass fibre barrel.

In 1956 Remington went one step further and brought out their gas-operated Model 58, the latest version of which is the Model 1100 which first appeared in 1963.

The name of Browning is still remembered, not only for the classic designs of the past but for a successful "two-shot" self-loading shotgun which was designed by Val. M. Browning, son of the famous John M. Browning. The Browning "Double Automatic" is a short recoil design, the rearward movement of the barrel being but $\frac{7}{8}$ in. Manufactured by FN this gun will only hold two cartridges and in line with modern trends it is offered in both standard and lightweight models, the lightweight having an action frame in light alloy.

Irrespective of the country of manufacture, nearly all the present day automatic shotguns are based on American ideas. A notable exception is the Italian Cosmi made by Rodolfo Cosmi of Ancona. With no disrespect intended, the Cosmi can be said to be the "Purdey" of the self-loading shotguns. It is available in 12- and 20-bore and the magazine is in the butt stock. The gun opens for loading with a top lever.

John Browning's five shot automatic of 1900 as made by F.N. of Belgium. This is an example in 20 bore of the finest work done by F.N. The engraving of a prehistoric hunting scene is by the renowned engraver F. Funken.

For all practical purposes the period under review has spanned a century and a half. During this period two significant changes have taken place. The first is a very real increase in the speed of loading and, of course, rate of fire, and the second is the influence of the machine tool in the production of sporting firearms. Here again there are two aspects, the first is the application of power to the tool, and the second, building skills into the tool.

However, because of the peculiarities of the way many people employ sporting firearms, weapons which were perfected a century ago are still being made and, perhaps even odder, some of the weapons made a century ago are still in use.

These eccentricities can be paralleled in so far as manufacture is concerned, high quality side-by-side double sidelocks are still made by techniques unchanged in essentials for decades, and self-loading shotguns are made by the most modern and up-to-date machine tools available.

The outline of the history of the sporting shotgun has been quickly sketched in; let us now look, more closely, at some of the important developments that took place during this period and, at the same time, have the odd sideways glance at some of the oddities that appeared, that even today still delight and intrigue us.

2

Flint Guns

Detached lock by Edwards.

Flint guns

The content of my articles over the years reflects to a great extent the interests of the readers, or to be more precise, those readers who write to me. Very little enthusiasm has been shown for flintlock weapons and this is no doubt due to the difficulty and expense of acquiring a flintlock shotgun today, coupled with an understandable reluctance to hazard a rare and consequently expensive gun by using it. For this reason little has been written on flintlocks in the series but these few articles have been selected to show that the subject was not entirely neglected.

A century and a half ago Thomas Oakleigh made a remarkably prophetic statement "Horsed mails and flintlocks will soon be forgotten, or remembered only to give a romantic interest to some tale of other times." Horsed mails are most certainly remembered on romantic Christmas Cards but Tom Oakleigh might have been a little surprised to have learned that people would continue to find pleasure, amusement, and interest in shooting flintlock weapons when full automatic weapons firing self-contained cartridges were available!

At the beginning of the nineteenth century, when flint guns were used for war and sport, much of the art of the gunmaker was of necessity devoted to the mechanical perfection of his gunlocks. On the gunlock depended the quickness of firing and with the appearance of the detonator the speed of ignition was dependent on the skill of the chemist who formulated the detonating powder. To combat the speed of the detonator or percussion lock, the makers of flintlocks had to use all their skill and wiles, and it is during the period of competition that the flintlock was raised to the peak of its perfection before being vanquished in the revolution which produced the percussion gun and then the breechloader.

With the flintlock, speedy and positive ignition depended on a number of factors. An important one, as we have mentioned, was the quality of the gunlock itself. Assuming sound materials and good workmanship, the "balance" or proportion of the springs in the lock were "of the utmost consequence". Here an important distinction between flintlocks and later locks has to be made. In the flint the term hammer was used to describe the "L" shaped component, the combined steel and pan-cover. Modern usage tends to use the term hammer for what was originally known as the cock. We still use the original terminology today when we speak of "cocking a gun".

Having cocked a flint gun, the release of the cock by pulling the trigger impels the flint forward in an arc. The tip of the flint, held in the jaws of the cock, strikes the top of the hammer and scrapes down the front of the steel, removing from the face small particles of hot metal. The whole of the hammer moves rearward uncovering the pan with its fine priming powder. Into this powder fall the incandescent particles of steel, resulting in the ignition of the priming and the subsequent ignition of the main charge.

The balance of the mainspring, which impels the cock forward, and the hammer spring, which tends to keep the hammer in its original position, are of the greatest importance. If the mainspring is too strong and the hammer spring too weak, the cock

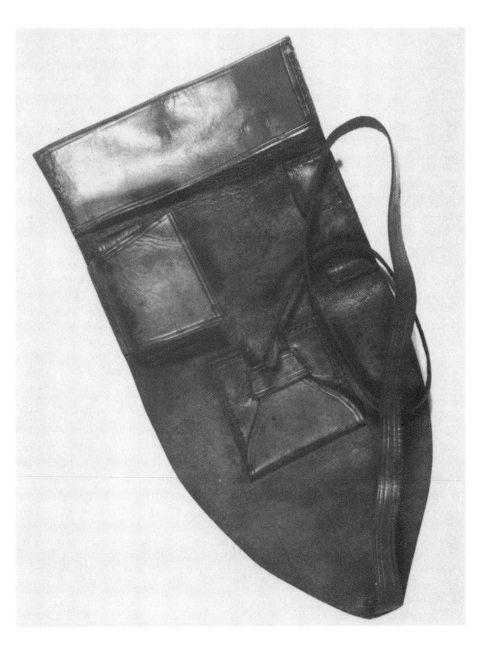

Leather wallets such as this were used throughout the muzzle-loading period to hold all the odd tools and gadgets needed by those who used flint or percussion ignition. If you are lucky you may find one still containing spare flints, turnscrews, etc., or a later one with nipple key and spare nipples.

is likely to fracture; if the position is reversed, the weak mainspring has insufficient force to drive back the hammer and again misfires will result. The temper of the face of the hammer or the steel is also of importance. If the steel is too soft it will be quickly cut into by the flint and if too hard little impression will be made and in either case too few "sparks" will result for effective ignition. If all is well most writers of the period advised their readers that the sparks produced "will be numerous, brilliant and accompanied by a whizzing sound".

I have listened with great care and with a continually disappointed anticipation for the "whizzing" sound. I fear that I must have lost the art of making whizzing sounds with my flintlocks. I have had a good record of absence of misfires but regret the absence of musical accompaniment. Essential to the success of the whole operation was the availability of good gunflints. In this country we have been fortunate in having an excellent supply which has served many generations of shooting men and still does.

The flints, carefully shaped, came from Brandon in Suffolk. The gunmaker and the flintnapper had done their job. Now it was the turn of the sportsman; he had to fit the flint correctly otherwise all the labours would have gone for naught. The flints had to be placed in the jaws of the cock with the flat side uppermost and they had to stand clear of the hammer and yet so adjusted that the flint would "throw" the hammer when the lock was fired. The modern shooter would find today that he needs something else – packing for the flint and for this purpose leather is best since lead strains the cock and linen cloth could retain a dangerous spark!

Hammers needed refacing from time to time but a regular occurrence was the need to change the flint. The true sportsman would carry a supply of spare flints with him and for convenience the flints were carried in a small leather purse, like the one illustrated on the previous page.

Most of the things used by the flintlock shooter have survived, guns, locks, flints etc., but the rarest is, perhaps, the little purse for the flints, mainly because today, few people would know what it was used for, if they came across an example by chance. If you do have one and have wondered what it was for, now you know. The flints to put in it can still be got; the black ones are best, from Brandon in Suffolk!

DOUBLE FLINTLOCK SHOTGUN

One of the most interesting guns which I have owned and used is a 24-bore flintlock shotgun with 31 inch barrels. As you can see from the illustration on pages 62 and 63, the barrels are marked Manton; London, and I have little reason to suppose that John Manton was not the maker.

Because of the name on the barrels this is where the chief interest lies. The barrels are numbered 2681 and from this I deduce that they date from about 1797. I have said that the barrels are 31 in. long – that includes the breeches – but the barrels proper are 30 in. They have a concave rib with the words "Manton · London", in gold reading from breech to muzzle and the plugs have two gold bands; first a thin band, then a thick one. The touch-holes are of gold.

London proof marks – each in a small oval – are to be found under the barrels, which are attached to the stock by means of the conventional hook breech and a single barrel securing bolt, the stock being protected by two small silver plates. The barrels have patent breeches, but these are not cut away as was later the case, so that the gun is fairly broad in the beam. The stock itself does not appear to be original, although it is correct in style, and the trigger guard is entirely in keeping with late eighteenth century practice.

Of greater interest is the fact that the locks do not bear the name Manton. This is regrettable, since the value of the gun would have been higher; instead, they bear the name McCrerick. Externally they appear to be of very good quality. Of a type known as "spur" cocks, the breast of the cock falls on the flash-pan fence and the pan is of the "rain-proof" type. There is a friction roller on the hammer spring. One has to remember that in the flintlock the hammer was the steel and pan cover – not the cock. The locks appear to be slightly later than the rest of the gun, both as regards stocking, furniture and breeching. Internally, they do not live up to outside appearances, and the quality of workmanship is not quite as high, although the locks are very quick and I have had few misfires when using the gun. Apart from the name on the outside of the lockplate they are devoid of any markings.

John, it will be recalled, was the elder of the two Mantons – John and Joseph – and he started in business in 1781. He signed himself Manton · London, whereas Joe signed himself Joseph Manton. Joe was undoubtedly a genius, while John was a superb craftsman, and both the brothers left a mark indelibly printed on the history of the British sporting shotgun. Who then was McCrerick? How did locks bearing his name get on to a gun with Manton barrels?

The most likely man to have made the locks is William McCrirrick of Irvine, who was in business as a gunmaker in that town about 1800. He was quite a character, for not only did he make guns and found a dynasty of gunmakers, he also invented a screw propeller in the days when ships propelled by steam used paddles. My best guess is that in those far-off days when materials cost more than a man's time, a Manton shotgun was damaged in some way. The locks could easily have been lost since it was the practice to keep them separate from the stock to reduce the risk of corrosion. After shooting, one removed the locks, gave them a good clean to remove the black powder fouling, and then kept them separate until the gun was ready for use again. I think the gun has also been restocked, probably when new locks were fitted. On the other hand McCrerick (the spelling changes) could have been handed a pair of Manton barrels, highly prized in those days, and merely told "make me a gun out of these".

I knew the last of the McCrirricks quite well. He had a gunshop in Kilmarnock and was the grandson of James McCririck (one "r"), who was the nephew of the original William. "James 1st" had a gunshop in Ayr but he was connected with the Irvine business since I have a snuff box with a concealed hinge made by James in 1829, which was given to me by "William III" in Kilmarnock some years ago.

I have used the Manton/McCrerick flint gun quite a number of times. A dram and a

Overleaf
Double flintlock gun by McCrirrick of Irvine, with barrels signed
"Manton, London".

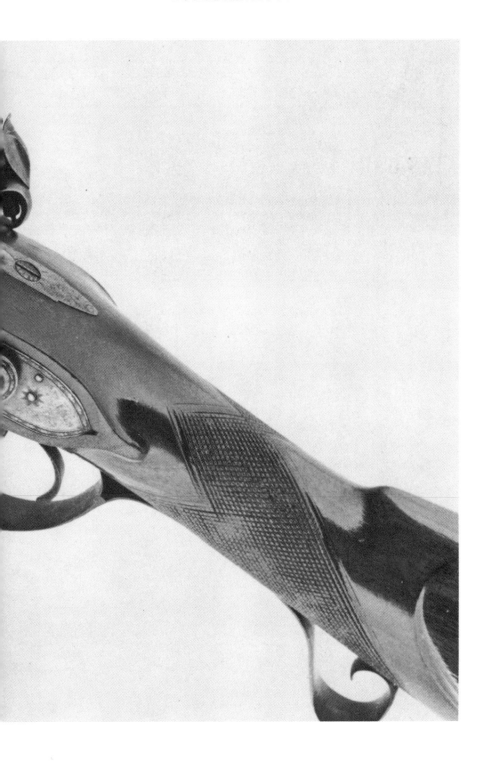

half of powder and $\frac{3}{4}$ ounces of shot seem to suit it nicely. I like this old gun as it reminds me of many a happy hour spent in the Kilmarnock shop talking about the old days with "William III", a most charming and truly delightful man. We could talk about guns for the sake of the gun in those days, for prices hadn't even started their ever-increasing upwards spiral that has taken the collecting of guns into the realms of high finance.

A DETACHED LOCK

Amongst the oddments relating to guns that I have managed to collect over the years are a number of what are called "detached locks". These are locks, some complete, others not, which have, for some reason or other, become detached from the firearm of which they were once a part.

There are wheel-locks, flintlocks and percussion locks and a selection of locks from pin- and central-fire guns and rifles. All have something of interest about them, the

Detached lock by Edwards.

The extremely high quality of this lock can be seen from the inside work. Note in particular the bridle.

craftsmanship, the name on the plate, or perhaps some technical innovation which, at the time the lock was made, marked an important turning point in the history of locks and lockwork.

One lock in particular never fails to arouse my continued interest. It does so for a number of reasons, some are pretty evident, the most important is not. From the illustration it will be seen that this is a flintlock. It is slightly over five inches in length, rather large for a pistol, so perhaps it originally came from a sporting gun. The name I. W. Edwards is engraved in capitals just in front of the cock and there are no other marks to be seen elsewhere. There are a number of gunmakers with the name "Edwards" listed but none with the initials I. W. so this line of research is a blank.

Whoever I. W. Edwards was he fitted locks of the finest quality to his wares. The engraving is minimal, the effect is obtained by line and shape. The cock is a masterpiece, every line is correct and the whole is most pleasing. There are little points to be observed. The screw which secures the feather spring is inserted from behind the lockplate as is the hinge pin for the steel and pan cover. This arrangement does not improve the mechanical efficiency of the lock but it certainly improves the external appearance.

One of the secrets in obtaining fast and positive ignition with a flintlock was to ensure the absence of friction as far as possible. This was done in a number of ways, one of which is well illustrated on the lock under discussion. Close examination of the photograph will show that there is a little wheel on the steel and pan cover which bears against the feather spring. The wheel bears against a hump on the free limb of the spring and provides initial resistance to the opening of the pan cover as the flint strikes the steel and then, once the steel is in motion, it is flicked back so ensuring that the sparks fall into the pan.

Behind that cock is a safety bolt which bolts the internal tumbler in the half cock position. Unusual on a lock of this type, an additional refinement also bolts the pan cover and the hole at the base of the steel into which the locking bolt enters is to be seen on the illustration of the inside of the lock.

The illustration is even more interesting since it must be remembered that although it was the practice to remove locks from the gun for reasonably frequent cleaning, the inside of the lock was not normally in view. Have a look at the bridle which supports the tumbler and sear. This is a beautiful piece of work and a joy to behold as is the finial on the mainspring which can be seen under the priming pan. Again, care is taken to eliminate friction where possible and the longer limb of the mainspring is linked with a swivel to the tumbler with this in view.

One could examine each part of this lock without finding fault and indeed, the only complaint is that the capstan screw which adjusts the top jaw of the cock has been damaged at some time in the past.

We now come to the important aspect of this lock, one of the main reasons why I look upon it with affection. It has been in my possession over twenty years. It came through the letterbox one day in a tobacco tin wrapped in brown paper. With it was a short note from a Mr. G. Lister of Putney who told me he had had it for years and was sending it to me. I wrote to Mr. Lister, for such acts are rare in this day and age when, too often, the value of an object is only of importance when translated into pounds. I have never met Mr. Lister and to this day I don't know why he chose me as the recipient of this really lovely lock. It was a truly delightful surprise when I received it and the passing of the years has served only to increase my pleasure of possession and, not surprisingly, my affection for the mysterious Mr. G. Lister.

"HAMMERLESS FLINTLOCK"

When one considers the amount of "top hamper" on a normal flintlock – the cock itself, the adjustable top jaw, the flint and the packing for the flint, the frizzen or hammer and the feather spring and, of course, the pan for the priming powder – the thought of a flint gun without all this machinery is somewhat strange.

If asked, most of us would say that the hammerless gun, whether a sporting gun, rifle or pistol, was an invention of the late nineteenth century. With one or two exceptions such a statement would be true, but it is those exceptions which can always be found in the world of guns which make life so full of surprises and so fascinating.

One has only to compare the pistol illustrated with a normal flintlock to realise how

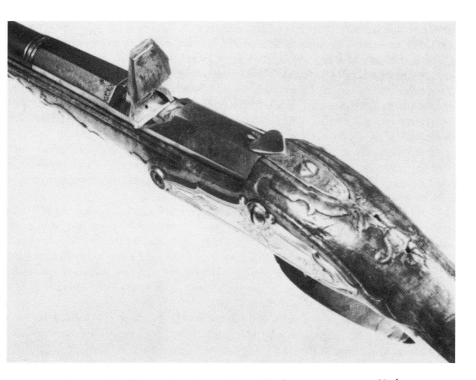

The tip of the flint can just be seen here with the pan cover open. Under is the pan itself, with a central vent for the ignition of the powder charge.

exceptionally clever was the gunsmith who invented and made this concealed lock. When this pistol is first seen the immediate reaction is to turn it over to look at the other side when one expects to find the usual inletting of the stock for the lockplate. One cannot help but think that here is a flintlock pistol which has had the lock removed! Both sides of the stock are the same, there is no lockplate but two sideplates, both identical, and a rather long trigger guard with two triggers. This and the odd triangular shaped piece of metal hinged to the rear of the barrel gives the game away, for this is no ordinary pistol and examples of this type of construction are extremely rare.

The pistol would be loaded with powder and ball from the muzzle in the normal manner. The steel and pan cover combined is then hinged upwards, uncovering the tip of the flint held in the jaws of what must, I suppose, be called a striker. The pan which is formed at part of the breeching of the barrel is then primed with powder and the lock cocked by pulling the front "trigger" to the rear. This draws back the flint against the pressure of a coil spring and, when cocked, the pan cover and steel are hinged downwards, closing the opening in the barrel extension so that the entire length of the barrel presents a smooth unbroken line.

If the rear trigger is now pressed, the flint, impelled by the coil spring moves forward until it strikes against the steel, which, since it is at an angle, is impelled upwards, opening the pan and allowing ignition of the priming to take place.

The pistol, one of a pair, was made by Fromery of Berlin in the mid-eighteenth century and the pistols, in addition to their most unusual lockwork, have nicely carved stocks and brass furniture. A pair of pistols with concealed box locks are to be found in the Hermitage Museum, Leningrad, which were made for the Empress Elizabeth I of

Close-up of the "tin box" which encloses the lock work with the lid open. The cocking lever, outside the "box", can be seen together with Copland's crest on the stock.

Russia and are unusual in that they are covered with green velvet. A fowling piece signed Stanislas Paczelt, Prag, with a concealed flintlock is in the collection of the Tower of London and perhaps the most remarkable of all this type of weapon can be seen in the Bavarian National Museum in Munich. This weapon is a double barrel fowling piece with the stock veneered with tortoiseshell and inlaid with silver. Unlike the Fromery pistols, the locks of this sporting gun are cocked by drawing back two

knobs, one on either side of the barrel, instead of a trigger cocking lever. All of these concealed lock flintlock weapons appear to have been made in Germany during the middle of the eighteenth century.

Nobody known to me has ever fired one of the weapons nor have I even come across a contemporary comment so we are in the dark as to how effective this type of lock was in normal use. Certainly, for normal everyday sporting use, there were doubtless drawbacks, the most likely of which would be fouling. We have to admit that we know very little about the concealed flintlock but these few examples serve once again to demonstrate that where firearms are concerned it is very rash to make a dogmatic statement, because somewhere or other is likely to be that one example which proves to be the exception to the rule.

"TIN BOX" GUN

Every now and again I come across something which is both intriguing and yet mystifying. This, of course, is one of the many reasons why my interest in firearms continues unabated because one never knows when the next "mysterious object" will appear.

One day, when in Dumfries, I took the opportunity of spending part of my lunch hour in the local museum. From past experience I know that many of the smaller local museums have a small collection of firearms amongst which are sometimes to be found items of considerable interest.

Such was the case in Dumfries. Here I found a most unusual weapon. As you can see on the previous page it is a single-barrel flintlock with two curious tin boxes enclosing the lockwork.

We will come back to the tin boxes in a moment. A single-barrel gun with two locks! The locks are quite plain and ordinary except that the cocks have an extended tail which protrudes through the enclosing box to the rear. One lock is on the left and the other on the right, the left-hand lock being mounted ahead of the right. This provides the clue! Two locks were not fitted merely to ensure that the charge was ignited but to ignite two charges one upon the other.

The use of superimposed loads is possibly the earliest method of obtaining a multi-shot firearm. It was delightful in its simplicity and, all too often, hazardous in actual use. Many of those made in the past were probably bought as a novelty but this is certainly not the case with this gun by Haugh since it is quite obvious that it was used, and very probably, on the Solway wildfowl.

The gun is signed J. Haugh, Dumfries, on top of the barrel. It is more than likely that it was, in fact, made by Haugh who, although not well known, has quite a few unusual weapons to his credit which have managed to survive the passing of the years. The gun can be dated about 1790 and bears an oval silver plate on the side of the stock bearing the inscription "Wm Copland of Collistoun Esq" and a crest. Copland came of a well-known Dumfriesshire family and Collistoun was an estate, with a mansion, in the parish of Dunscore. Whether or not the gun was originally made with the lockwork enclosed is difficult to say but I rather doubt it.

I should like to think that William Copland bought this unusual gun from Haugh of Dumfries, and after some initial misgivings liked it so much that he took it back to Haugh and asked him to make certain improvements which would permit him to use the gun in bad weather. For a sporting merchant of Dumfries to buy such an unusual gun in the first place indicates that he was of a rather experimental turn of mind and well able to deal with the facetious and possible downright rude comments of his friends when seen out shooting with his "tin box" gun.

With the pans primed and the cocks drawn half back, the lids of the two boxes could be closed. When ready to shoot the "tails" attached to the cocks are pressed down drawing back the cocks; William Copland of Collistoun would have two shots as fast as he could pull the single trigger.

This gun is indeed both mystifying and intriguing, not so much in itself for we know how it works. The addition of the cocking tails to the flint cocks coupled with the use of protective tin boxes makes the gun even more unusual, possibly unique, but I, for one, would dearly like to know more about J. Haugh, Gunmaker of Dumfries and his equally interesting customer who so proudly placed his name in silver on the stock.

3

The Percussion Gun

This is the third model Forsyth "Roller primer" fitted to a duelling pistol. The pistol has, in fact, three locks: flint, roller primer and early cap lock. The pistol dates from 1805, the lock from c. 1820.

The percussion gun

The percussion period can be fairly said to have opened with Forsyth's invention of the "detonator". His patent of 11 April, 1807 describing "an advantageous method of discharging firearms" was momentous and although the principle was not widely adopted because of the cost and difficulty of making the roller locks, the company formed by Forsyth made guns to the very highest standards. Many of the roller primer locks were later converted to cap locks and some weapons will be found with up to three types of lock, all interchangeable! High quality flint lock weapons were converted to the roller primer lock using loose primer powder and roller primer weapons were converted to cap lock. Joseph Manton patented his pellet lock in 1816 and a tube lock in 1818. By 1820 the hold that Forsyth had exercised on the gun trade by his patent and spirited defence of it was lessening and licences were being granted for the manufacture of percussion locks. Other makers sought to evade the Forsyth master patent by variations and others patented "improvements". The Forsyth roller lock worked well when kept clean and properly adjusted. If neglected, largely due to the extremely corrosive nature of the primer powder, it would give trouble.

Amid the profusion of pill, pellet, patch and tube locks, and, of course, the use of loose powder in a magazine, one system emerged, the cap lock. Who invented the cap lock is likely to remain a mystery but it is interesting to realise that this little cap, now with an anvil, is to be found as the means of ignition of today's central-fire cartridges!

The 1820s saw the emergence of the cap lock and by 1830 it was the dominant system. Flint guns continued to be used for the next 50 years and tube locks were favoured for special purposes such as wildfowling guns, but "percussion" guns had been brought to the height of perfection before the mid-nineteenth century and in spite of the development of the breechloader in one of its many and varied forms, muzzle-loading guns did not suddenly vanish, although for sporting use one could say that 1870 saw the end of the fashionable period.

The percussion period brought with it patent litigation, claim and counter claim and the promotion of a number of different ways in which the basic principle of a detonating compound could be applied to the task of igniting the powder charge of a sporting gun. Some of these systems and the guns to which they were fitted are described in greater detail in the chapters which follow.

Today's modern shotguns, rifles and pistols are percussion firearms. All are fired by the ignition of fulminating mixtures, the properties of which have been known for a long time. These properties were such as to cause injury and disfigurement to many an experimenter, and it was an intrepid man who dared to unlock the secrets of these choleric compounds.

Many of the fulminating compounds had been made during the seventeenth and eighteenth centuries. Work was carried out to see if these interesting, if irascible, materials could be used as a propellant.

It was a Scottish clergyman, the Rev. Alexander John Forsyth of Belhelvie,

Aberdeenshire, who first thought to use fulminates as igniters rather than propellants and his first patent was taken out in 1807. Forsyth was born in 1768 and on his father's death in 1790 he was given the living at Belhelvie where he continued as minister until his death in 1843. His interests were not altogether unpredictable. He was interested in chemistry, mechanics and similar pursuits of a scientific nature and he was also a keen fowler.

Legend has it that it was the birds he missed due to the flash from the priming of his flintlock that first made him wonder if there was not a better and simpler way of igniting the charge of powder in his fowling-piece. By 1805 he had made a successful lock which was offered to the Government of the day but after a further year of experiment, political changes forced Forsyth to abandon any further effort to interest the military in his invention.

Forsyth, having obtained his patent in 1807, set up shop at No. 10 Piccadilly and started making long guns and pistols which used his percussion lock. Forsyth was not a gunmaker and he persuaded James Purdey, then at Joseph Manton's, to join him and supervise his workshop. Purdey, of course, went on to even higher things, founding the firm which today still bears his name.

The lock dismantled, the cylindrical roller screws into the lock plate; the platinum touch-hole of the original barrel has not been altered to allow for the original flint lock to be used when required.

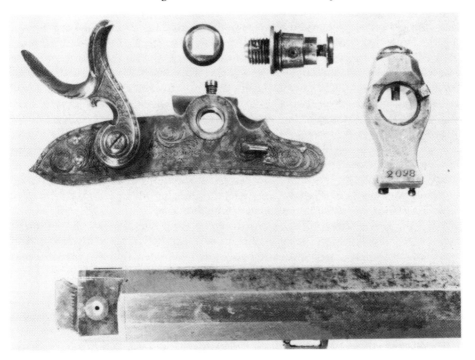

The best known of the Forsyth detonating locks is his so-called "scent bottle" lock, the name being derived from the shape of the magazine which held the priming powder.

The Forsyth scent bottle lock is an example of the rather rare interchangeable type of lock which, as the description implies, was intended for use on firearms where, if necessary, the owner could revert to the use of his flintlock should anything happen to the detonator lock or even if he ran out of a supply of detonating compound.

The internal mechanism of the lock is quite conventional although, as one would expect, it is of very high quality. The lock plate is pierced by a hole into which is screwed a tapered steel plug. The end of the plug butts against the vent of the barrel when the lock is attached to the pistol so forming a continuous channel from the inside of the barrel, through the vent, through the plug and connecting with a small depression in the taper section of the plug. The scent bottle magazine fits on to the taper section of the plug and is retained by a washer and a large pan-headed screw. Not only does the scent bottle contain a magazine for the fulminate priming in the bottom section, there is also the firing pin in the top section. The pin protrudes into the central cavity of the magazine.

Priming powder is introduced by means of a sliding cover in the base of the magazine, the cover having what we would call today an "explosion disc". This is a little horn plug retained by friction, the purpose of which is to provide an easy escape for the "explosion" should the contents of the magazine be accidentally detonated. Without this feature the sliding cover would be blown off.

With the magazine loaded or charged, the hammer is brought to half cock and the scent bottle rotated through 180 degrees. At this point the port in the magazine coincides with the depression in the plug and a small quantity of priming powder is deposited into the tiny "pan" of the plug. The magazine is then turned back through 180 degrees so that the firing pin is then opposite the primed pan. When the hammer falls, the pin ignites the priming, the flash from which passes through the centre channel of the plug, through the vent of the barrel and ignites the main charge of back powder.

In order to work safely and with regularity, the Forsyth lock had to be made to close tolerances and it was expensive to produce. Indeed, a good quality flintlock fowler could be bought for the price of a Forsyth lock alone but in spite of the cost of the lock and the relatively high cost of the priming powder, the user of the new system had much to be thankful for, released as he was from the tyranny of flint and steel and the annoyance of having to prime the pan and adjust his flint.

Although the use of loose priming compound gave way to the little copper percussion cap, Forsyth was the first man to demonstrate that fulminating compounds could be used effectively to discharge rifles, pistols and shotguns and his contribution to the "art of gunnery" is somewhat belatedly commemorated by a tablet in the Tower of London, placed there as a memorial to Forsyth in 1929.

MORE ABOUT FORSYTH AND HIS LOCK

There has always been considerable interest shown in the work of the Rev. Alexander

John Forsyth, Minister of Belhelvie, Aberdeenshire and one aspect of this is the attitude of sportsmen of the period to the use of the detonating compound which in the Forsyth lock displaced the use of flint and steel and brought firearms into a completely new era, literally with a bang. For the proper appreciation of this, try and visualise a flintlock machine-gun! Flintlock repeating rifles there had been, but they were for the curious and the connoisseur.

Arguably, the invention of percussion ignition was one of the most significant events in the history of firearms and it is interesting that it was not one of the great London gunmakers but an obscure Scottish clergyman who rightly claims responsibility for this innovation.

The history of Forsyth's work has been well documented and well written about over the years starting with a book on his work published in 1909 and subsequently reprinted in 1955. Later, in 1969, came the definitive work of the subject *Forsyth & Co., Patent Gunmakers* by W. Keith Neal and D. H. L. Back.

A question often asked is how did the sportsman of the period cope with Forsyth's irascible compound, for on this subject the literature is remarkably quiet.

Oddly enough the later percussion cap has a number of well-documented accidents due to the early caps being too brittle and bits flying off into people's eyes or faces.

But let us start with the detonating compound. The chemistry books tell us that it was Charles Howard FRS who reported upon a "new fulminating mercury" which he had discovered and it was not long before the spectacular properties of mercury fulminate ($Hg(ONC)_2$) became apparent and, indeed, Howard was seriously injured in the course of his researches. Silver fulminate was known in the seventeenth century but was "far too sensitive to be touched once made", though it was used in small quantities in toy fireworks. It now seems that Forsyth originally used a mixture of potassium chlorate and that this material on impact started an explosive reaction with the production of a hot flame which, in turn, ignited the charge of the powder. Forsyth first thought of the use of this new class of explosive as a propellant and according to family history these early experiments resulted in an explosion which blew the Rev. gentleman from his workshop.

The manufacture of the entire class of "initiating explosives" is one which was fraught with hazard and even in later years more than one factory making percussion caps suffered from accidents caused by these sensitive materials. Having produced an effective percussion compound Forsyth then turned his mind to the manufacture of a lock which could be attached to a gun and so use the igniting compound in a useful manner. Success came in 1805.

Then to London and abortive work in the Tower followed by the establishment of the Forsyth Patent Gun Company at No. 10 Piccadilly, London. Sportsmen were very chary of the new system although it offered many advantages and most kept the original locks if the percussion gun they used had been converted. One such man returned his Forsyth gun to have the percussion locks replaced by flintlocks since he had experienced a number of misfires.

In favour of Forsyth it must be stated that many of the complaints against the guns of misfires were entirely due to bad management and lack of cleaning. Innes, gunmaker of Edinburgh who made Forsyth locks under licence, referred to the

problem of misfires and was of the opinion that this was due to the majority of sportsmen being unable to deal with the intricacies of the new lock.

That the lock required skilled workmen to make it was undeniable for the whole history of the company is strewn with complaints against workmen and constant vigilance was needed to ensure that the locks were made to the closest of tolerances. One or two accidents are mentioned but the most widely reported was that to Sir James Pulteney who was severely injured when shooting on 20 April, 1811. He survived but six days, and the press reported that the accident had been caused by the explosion of a flask of oxygenated muriate of potash. Forsyth countered the bad publicity by publishing a letter in the *Sporting Magazine* which stated that the accident had been caused by the explosion of a flask of black powder and was in no way related to the use of the patent Forsyth lock.

To learn a little more about Forsyth and his lock and the "chemical powder", we have to turn, as always, to Col. Peter Hawker. Some interesting facts also come from *The Shooter's Guide* (B. Thomas, London 1816, 5th. edn.), the first edition of which tells how the author "saw the new-invented gunlock in the shop of the inventor in the

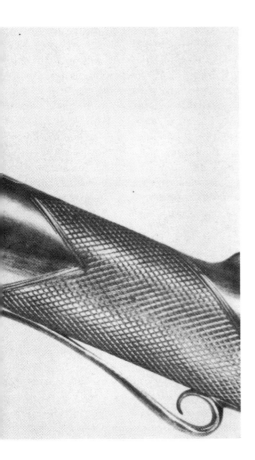

The earlier type of Forsyth Roller primer or "scent bottle" lock fitted to a double gun by McDermott of Dublin. Locks c. 1815.

month of March 1811". We are given the receipt for the "chemical powder, oxymuriate of potash 9 parts, sulphur 1½ parts, charcoal 1 part". The mixture produced a stronger flash than fulminate of mercury but it was more corrosive and it was corrosion that caused much of the troubles with the lock mechanism.

In 1816 Thomas stated that he had still not used it and advised sportsmen that if they wished to use the new lock they need not be at the expense of buying a new fowling piece for the purpose as "it may be applied to any gun in the same manner as the common lock: the price of a single lock is eight guineas".

Hawker, in the first edition of his *Instructions*, warmly recommended the Forsyth lock. By the time the fourth edition appeared in 1825 the copper cap was supreme and the Forsyth lock was not mentioned. It is of interest to record, however, that instructions are still given for making detonating powder but this time one has to assume that this is for use with copper caps or patches.

I recall recapping a number of rather rare fired cases from which I have removed the caps, removed the dent in the cap, introduced the priming composition, covered this with a small piece of tissue and then reassembled the cartridge. Whether or not it was the practice for those far away from the centre of things to make their own detonating powder from one of the several formulae available and then to reprime their fired caps I cannot say but it certainly was possible, given the required skill and care, to make the "chemical powder", for use in the Forsyth lock. Some people appear to have used a small copper powder flask for the priming, but a wooden container was thought more suitable. I had in my possession some years ago a flintlock pistol which also had a Forsyth lock and a later pellet lock. The pistol was fired with all three types of ignition system without trouble and I still have a small quantity of the "initiatory explosive" if an opportunity should arise in the future.

Possibly one reason why the literature is silent on explosions and disasters with Forsyth locks is that relatively few were used and those made were discarded when the alternative system became available. The Forsyth Company started in business in 1808 and in less than 20 years was making guns firing copper caps.

THE DEVELOPMENT OF THE DETONATOR

The use of detonating mixture for the ignition of firearms began with the successful adoption of Forsyth's invention for use with sporting firearms in the opening years of the nineteenth century. The use of loose fulminating powder was attended with several difficulties, not the least being the high cost of the detonating locks.

As an alternative to using loose powder in a dispensing magazine the priming could be made up in special containers. One method which was adopted was to make up the correct amount of powder in a paper patch, not dissimilar to the caps still used today for toy pistols. The top illustration shows the type of lock used with these early patches; this is the type sold by Westley Richards and patented by him in 1821. This lock was originally intended for use with loose fulminate powder in a magazine but the small pan cover shown in the illustration could be substituted for the magazine and the lock used with patches. Quite a range of patch locks were made but the difficulty of handling the patches and their relative fragility resulted in their being displaced by other means of ignition. A more robust alternative, and one which had considerable success, was the tube lock. One of the best of the tube locks was patented by Westley Richards in 1831 and the general design of the lock and the type of primer can be seen in the lower illustration.

The tubes for Westley Richards guns were inserted into a nipple or touch-hole, the upper end remaining proud due to a collar around the tube. The tube was ignited by a blow on the end by the hammer. Col. Hawker, that intrepid arbiter of fashion, strongly recommended Westley Richards "primers" stating "that he had never known

Top right

The upper illustration shows the Westley Richards patch lock and underneath is his tube lock showing the special type of primer employed.

Bottom right

Tube lock double gun by Moore of London. Note the spring clips to hold the tube in place and the shield on the hammer nose.

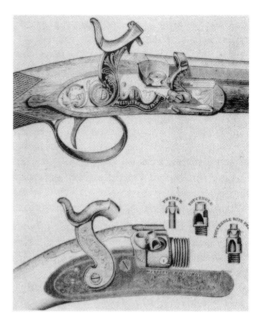

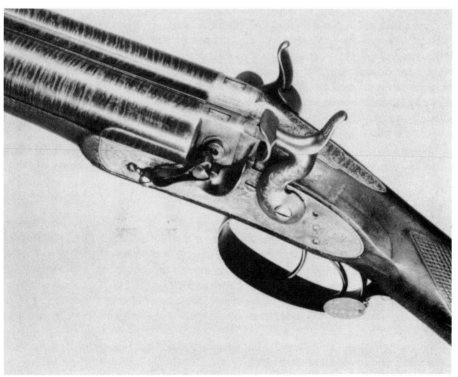

it to fail," and, in fact, the most important feature of the tube or "primer" ignition system was its certainty.

As a further alternative, the tube could be inserted into the side of the breech and secured by a snap cover. This system was first put forward by Joseph Manton in 1818 but there was the disadvántage that the tube could come flying out of the gun with some considerable force when detonated and several alternative schemes were put forward. The illustration shows a tube lock gun made by Moore of London which shows the little spring on the lock plate that held the primer against the anvil. The problem of bits of tube flying out from the side of the gun to the annoyance and perhaps injury of a bystander was not solved by this system, although Charles Lancaster patented a slightly different type of tube primer which was somewhat safer in this respect.

The most astonishing thing about the percussion nipple and cap which was to sweep away tubes, pellets, pill, tapes and all the other types of priming, is that we know less concerning its origins than we do about some of the more unusual and certainly far less widely adopted ignition systems that briefly appeared, flashed and vanished into obscurity.

The nipple, pivot or peg certainly appeared before the cap. We know with some certainty who first *patented* the use of the cap, namely a Frenchman, Prelat. We also know that Prelat was in business patenting new ideas in France, and had, in fact, obtained a patent in 1810 for a copy of the Forsyth lock patented in Britain in 1807.

The claimants for the honour of *inventing* the humble copper cap which, it must be remembered, is still in use today, tucked away in the base of every centre-fire cartridge, were numerous. They were, as Captain Lacy, writing in 1842 put it, "as of old, there were contending cities for the honour of having given birth to Homer". Lacy mentioned the claims of Egg, Hawker and Purdey. Yet another claimant was Joshua Shaw of America. Shaw was granted a United States patent in 1822 and in 1824 Samson Davis was granted a British patent for "improvements to guns" which mentions the use of "the percussion cap".

Prelat certainly seized the opportunity of patenting the copper cap before anyone else, but who first thought of the idea?

PERCUSSION LOCKS

Mr. Taylor of Preston was one of my visitors at the Game Fair and he brought with him a detached lock. This is just a slightly pedantic way of saying that he had a gun lock without the rest of the weapon, and he wanted to know something about it: its history, origins and any other matters of interest that I could tell him. In cases such as this it is a bit difficult to know what to say. It can vary from, "Yes, you have an interesting lock. It's percussion, nineteenth century and European", and leave things there.

For many people this is enough but I had the feeling that Mr. Taylor wanted more detail. I told him I would photograph the lock and then write it up at a future date, and hope that the article produced would provide him with enough information either to

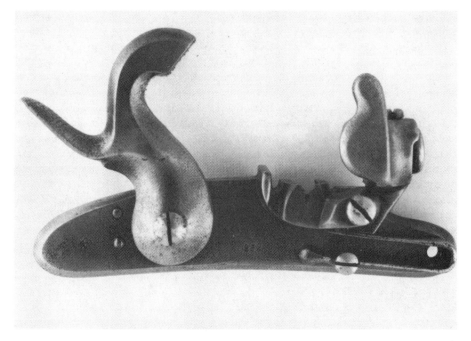

External view of the "Austrian" lock with the hammer at full cock.

satisfy his curiosity completely or at least show him where to go for further information.

All of this supposed that I would be able to take a reproducable photograph with a hand-held camera and in what are not always ideal conditions. In fact I have been giving much thought to a portable outdoor studio set-up which would give me the sort of photographs I need of guns brought to me at the Game Fair, but as yet I haven't thought about the other things I get to photograph, such as detached locks!

However, back to Mr. Taylor's lock. It is unusual since it has a hinged part which lifts up, and unlike our locks, it also lacks a nipple upon which to place a cap. Those who have studied percussion locks will know that as well as caps, all sorts of other methods have been used to contain the detonating powder. We have had locks like the original Forsyth lock which employed loose powder in a special magazine, the "scent bottle lock", and we have had pill, pellet, patch, tube and tape locks.

The lock illustrated is known to some people as an Austrian lock and this is, I suppose, a correct description. However, it is more accurately known as an Augustin lock and it is additionally identified as the Model 1842.

The Augustin lock is a "tube" lock and this method of containing the percussion powder was first used by Manton in 1818. In Europe Giuseppe Console designed a lock which was employed by the Austrians and later improved by Major General Vincent Augustin, as the "Model 1842".

The lock was made in the Imperial and Royal State Arms Factory (KuK Staatliche Gewehrfabrik) of Vienna and this may account for the Arms impressed on the lock behind the hammer. The significance of the number, other than perhaps it is a serial, is unknown.

One of the directors of the factory was Vincenz Augustin and lock parts appear to have been made by a great many firms and gunsmiths all over Austria. Between 1831 and 1844 the major powers adopted the percussion cap locks for military purposes, and only Austria, with the Console and later Augustin locks, was the exception, employing the tube lock. It is of interest to recall that the Manton tube lock had been tried out by the British Government in 1820 but had been rejected.

The Augustin lock was made in considerable quantities and many military firearms fitted with this lock will be encountered. A good number were exported to America and some appear to have been used by both the North and South in the Civil War; certainly "antique" dealers bought large numbers after the Second World War, and most of these found their way to America. To the collector of military muzzle-loading weapons, the Austrian "tube lock" of 1842 is both an interesting and well-made item.

THE CONVERSION

One type of shotgun which you rarely see today is the conversion. True, there are people who purchase a standard double 12 and then decide to have the looks improved. Work of this sort can include the refinishing of the woodwork, alterations of the trigger pulls and perhaps some reworking of the trigger guard to remove the sharp edges. The appearance of the barrels can be improved by some extra work and a re-blue job but essentially we still have the same gun with the same features.

As an alternative the owner of a machine-made pump or automatic shotgun can have new stock fitted, ventilated rib added and various other "custom" accessories are available to "improve" his gun. Again, there has been no basic alteration to the function of the weapon.

This was not so in years gone by. The owner of a single barrel percussion Jones shotgun bought a flintlock. A fine weapon it is as well. The barrel is 46 in. long and the gun is 62 in. overall. Although octagonal at the breech, the barrel becomes round at about the end of the fore end and, despite its length and weight, it is well balanced and the proportions of barrel stock and lock are well suited.

At the breech end of the barrel the original flint touch hole or vent has been drilled and tapped for a blanking off screw. The original flintlock lock plate has been retained but the pan has been removed and the plate smoothed away so that the loss is not too noticeable. One thing has not been filled in and that is the little hole at the front of the lock where the feather spring for the pan cover and steel fitted. Very obvious is the new hammer. The flint cock has been discarded and because of the method of conversion from flint to percussion the hammer has the nose bent over so that it can strike the nipple which has been fitted at an angle into the breech plug.

The conversion is neat, requires the minimum amount of work and is practical in that ignition of the charge is good and misfires, I have found, are rare. The alternative

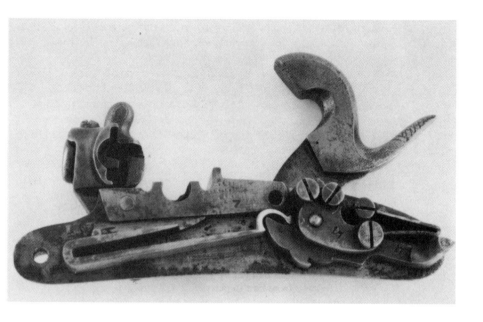

Inside the "Austrian" lock, illustrating the complex arrangement for
retaining the primer.

method would have been to fit a round drum into the vent and then a nipple could be
screwed into the drum. In this case such a conversion would have been a bit ungainly
and ignition perhaps not quite so sure. A more expensive method would have been to
have made a complete new breech plug. Unwarranted I think since in practice the
method that was employed served well for many years, since this gun was in use for
wildfowling until 1939. It could still be used for this purpose so that the conversion
was an entirely practical method of keeping the gun in service and overcoming what
we today would call "technological obsolescence".

What other conversions were there? Well, I think that the next important class was
the conversion from muzzle-loading to breechloading but, in view of the few which
have survived, I don't think that such conversions were always entirely satisfactory.
One did have most of the expensive bits of the gun, the locks, the barrels and the stock
and as long as the labour costs were low conversions of this type, which involved a
great deal of work, were a practical proposition.

Most conversions were from muzzle-loading to pinfire, some direct to central fire
but then there were a large number of guns converted from pin to central fire.

Yet another desirable feature of the central fire breechloader was ejection as
opposed to mere extraction and this was yet another conversion that was carried out. I
don't know of any hammer guns converted to hammerless but it is something that
might have happened. I always thought that Needham's needle fire shotgun must have

Single barrel percussion shotgun by Jones showing the method of
conversion from flint to percussion cap ignition.

been converted to central-fire by someone and until the last Game Fair lacked solid
evidence of my beliefs, but such a conversion was produced so perhaps somewhere
there is a hammer gun converted to hammerless!

One class of gun we have not mentioned so far is the conversion of a conversion, or a
reconversion. As the cost of flintlock weapons continues to rise one source previously
ignored has now been tapped. The flint guns that were converted to percussion. It's not
all that difficult to convert them back to flint and much of the gun is original.

So, if you are a collector and the flint shotgun that you have been waiting for all your
life turns up just check that you are buying an original, an original everything that is,
because if it had been converted back from percussion to "original" flint then the price
should be a little less!

A CONVERTED MANTON

As most shooting people know there were two important Mantons, John and Joseph.
John, the elder brother, worked for a time for Twigg, the famous gunmaker and then
set up on his own at 6 Dover Street in 1781. John Manton's output of firearms was
greater than that of his brother in both volume and variety. Of equal importance was
the output of "gunmakers" from the Dover Street premises, men who served their time
and worked for John Manton before setting up on their own account. Such men were
to found firms which later gained world wide reputations and not the least of them was
the firm of Joseph Manton, Joseph setting up on his own in 1789.

Inevitably the question arises, who built the best guns? Was it John or Joseph? I have never been able to make up my mind on this point. A decision is made and then the next Manton gun I have the opportunity of seeing appears to be nicer than my memory of the last one. If one is John Manton and the other Joe then one or the other comes out top of the poll until the next opportunity arises for me to again change my mind. Irrespective of who was the better gunmaker, both the Mantons had a decisive effect on British gunmaking not because of a single important or revolutionary invention but because of their influence on style and their insistence on quality.

The Manton illustrated overleaf is a double nominal 12-bore percussion shotgun made by John Manton and Son, Dover Street, in 1820. As originally made it would have been a flintlock with a spur or reversed "C" style of cock and "V" pans. At some time subsequent to manufacture this gun was converted from flintlock to percussion. The original breech plugs, with their cut-away sloping sides, would have been removed to be replaced by the percussion breech plugs now fitted. The slight chamfer on the side of the barrel can be seen just in front of the new breeching and, of course, the most noticeable thing about this gun is the hen-toed hammers.

From the side the hammers do not appear unduly unusual. They are, in fact, early percussion style hammers developed from the Forsyth pattern. There is one very important difference where the hammer nose strikes. In the Forsyth lock the hammer nose does not have to be "hen-toed" since the Forsyth "scent bottles" were mounted alongside the barrels. In the case of the Manton the percussion nipples are inset; they lie nearer to the centre line of the barrels and the hammer nose has to be turned inward in order to strike the nipple or pivot correctly. Turning the hammer nose in this fashion overcomes the problem without any technical difficulty but the result, from an aesthetic viewpoint, is not so satisfactory.

Those of you who have handled percussion shotguns will probably be able to recall how this problem was overcome. It was a problem since the "hen-toed" style did not survive, and a completely new style of percussion hammer was developed which was far neater and more in keeping with the line of the gun. This ability to adapt to technical innovation, to create new shapes and patterns which pleased the eye, was undoubtedly one of the reasons why gunmaking in nineteenth century Britain rose to the heights that it did.

Have a look at the top view of the Manton and pay particular attention to the hammers. If they do not appear slightly odd to you read no further. If they do, think how you would go about altering the shape to improve the appearance. Later we shall have a look at how this was done by the gunsmith and how a new style was evolved. It is, I agree, a small point. The gun will not and did not shoot any better, it was not easier to load or fire and was not cheaper to make but I think that you will agree, it looked better.

SCOTT PERCUSSION SHOTGUN

One of the most interesting aspects of writing is the way one article prompts comment from an interested reader and starts a whole chain of interconnected thoughts.

As a result of an article on Daniel Ross of Edinburgh I received a most interesting

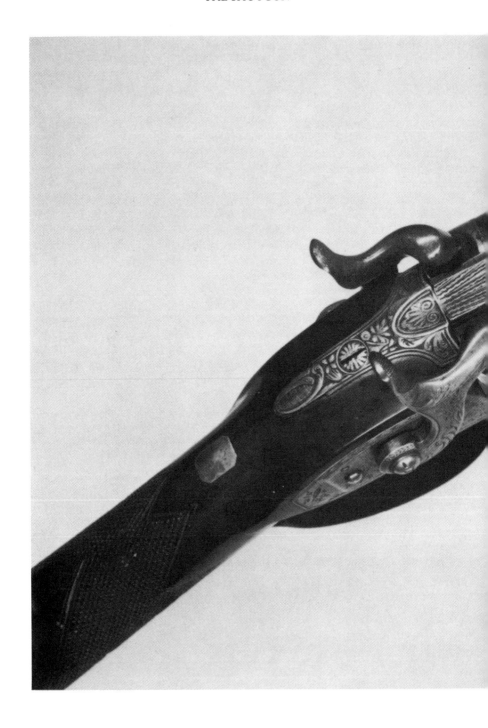

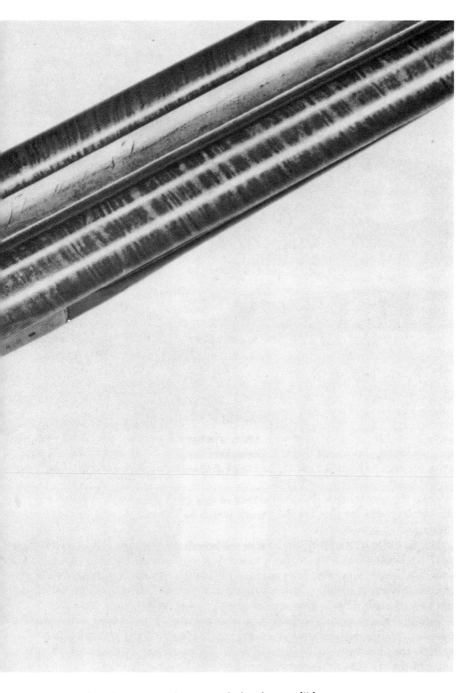

The John Manton shotgun with the "hen toed" hammers.

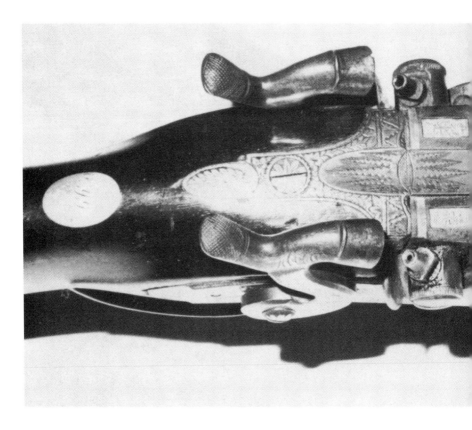

letter from Mr. H. J. Walker and, later, a series of photographs of his fine Scott shotgun. Scott was one of the first gunmakers listed in Edinburgh and dates back to 1793. He was listed in several of the 1804 Edinburgh directories and appears to have ceased business in or around 1836.

From the general style and appearance of this gun I would date it about 1820 and Mr. Walker tells me that the only work which he has had done is to re-brown the rather fine 20-bore barrels.

Behind the barrels proper can be seen the breech plugs and on top of each plug is a gold "cartouche" with the maker's name. Screwed into the plugs is the conversion system adopted by the man who changed the ignition system from flint to percussion cap, for this was originally a flintlock shotgun. When this conversion was carried out is not easy to say but the system employed was one of the simplest.

In effect, the original flint cock was removed and replaced by a new percussion hammer. The battery and steel or, as it was then known, the "hammer" was removed entirely together with the frizzen spring or feather spring. Here we can already see some of the problem of nomenclature, since for the same "L-shaped" piece of metal against which the flint strikes we now have three names.

The name used in 1820 was hammer. When it became worn it was re-steeled and so

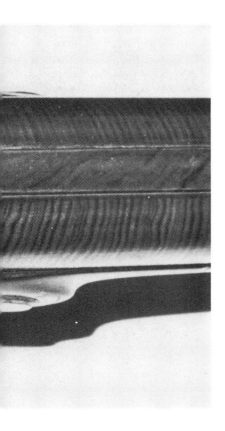

Double shotgun converted from flint to percussion by the "drum and nipple" method.

we have the second name "steel and pan-cover" for the combined components of the lock. Today the tendency is to call this component "the combined steel and pan-cover". The Americans use the term "frizzen" or "frizzel" and this might have been derived from the French "fusil" or even "frizz" meaning sputter, the noise the priming powder made on ignition. The term "hammer" would go out of use because of the confusion with the later use of this word for the percussion cock and, of course, the centre-fire hammer. Call it what you will, this part of the lock was removed and a new striker or cock or hammer fitted.

The touch hole or vent in the breech plug was enlarged and a short cylindrical piece screwed into a hole. To the side of the cylinder was attached a percussion "pivot" or nipple which would accommodate the percussion cap. This was arranged so that it could be struck by the face of the hammer when the flash from the cap would pass through the nipple and the cylinder into the breeching of the gun.

Such conversions exist today in quite reasonable numbers although there is a tendency for converted flint guns to be converted back to flint from percussion because of the higher value. This should be guarded against if you contemplate buying an expensive "refinished" flint gun. Alternatives to the "drum and nipple" system were many, from a complete re-build, so that the "new" percussion gun was almost indistinguishable from the contemporary original, to a system where the nipple was screwed directly into the breech plug and a curious "canted" hammer fitted.

The system used on the David Scott gun was fairly typical and the illustration shows how this was carried out. I always wonder whether or not the original owner ordered the conversion to be carried out or was it the second or third owner? Certainly, in the days when the cost of labour was low, this was the way to be up to date by having father's gun converted instead of having to buy a new one.

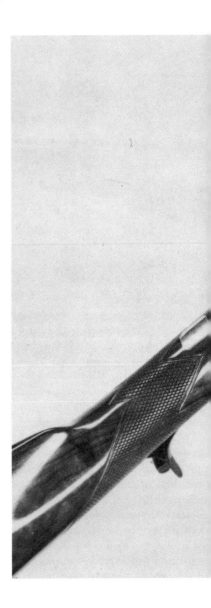

Double percussion rifle by McLaughlan of Edinburgh. Unlike shotguns many rifles saw little use in this country and this example is "mint" just as it left the Edinburgh shop all those years ago.

THE PERCUSSION HAMMER

I asked you to have a look at the hammers used for the conversion of the Manton shotgun and if, particularly from the top, you saw anything odd about their design or shape.

    I felt that many of you would be of the opinion that the pronounced inward curve,

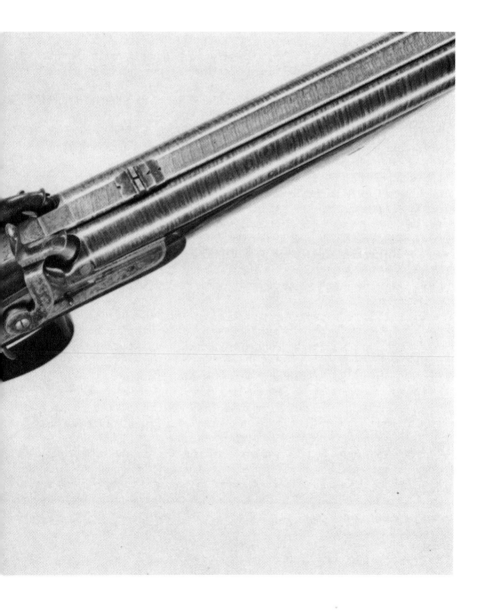

or what I called a "hen-toed" look, was unusual and slightly detracted from the appearance of the gun.

It was pointed out that these hammers were early percussion hammers and owed much in their general design to the hammers employed on the Forsyth locks. Since the original Forsyth hammers acted against the strikers mounted on the scent-bottle magazine and since the magazine was alongside the barrel, the hammer nose was straight. With the later type of percussion nipple mounted in the breeching, very nearly at the centre-line of the barrel, it became necessary to curve the hammer nose inwards.

To me, no matter how gracefully this inwards curve is arranged, the end result looks clumsy and conveys the impression of inadequate expediency. It was at this point that I invited those whose interest was aroused to attempt to design a suitable shape or style of hammer which could be fitted to a similar design of gun and which would have a more pleasing appearance.

I promised to show an example of how the majority of gunmakers tackled the problem and since it is rather difficult to describe in words I hope that the illustration will serve to show the design changes which took place and which were generally adopted, and leave it to you to judge whether or not the accepted style was an improvement on the earlier design.

The example which I have chosen to illustrate a typical percussion style of hammer is a double rifle by MacLaughlan of Edinburgh. This rifle is mid-nineteenth century and is in "as new" condition. Compare the three-quarter side view which clearly shows the hammers with the similar view of the Manton. You will notice that the hammer noses are straight and lie parallel to each other. How, then, has this been done? The answer can be seen when we look at the rifle from just along the comb of the stock and it can be seen clearly how the whole top of the hammer has been curved inwards. On the Manton hammers only the nose was curved and this, to me at least, was very obvious.

With the MacLaughlan and other percussion guns of the period the whole of the top of the hammer is curved inwards, but unless you look closely at the hammer from the rear, or, even better, remove the hammer from the lockplate, this inward curve is not noticeable and tends to be ignored by the observer who is more aesthetically satisfied by the symmetry of the two hammers with their parallel noses.

You may not agree with me that the later design of percussion hammer is better looking. You may, in fact, consider that the whole exercise has been a waste of time and the shape of hammers is of little consequence, provided that they can be cocked easily by the thumb and fire the gun when required.

Whatever your point of view it is nevertheless a fact that the style of percussion hammer did change and by observance one can date a percussion gun by the hammer style. A further change in style was dictated by technical considerations with the appearance of the pinfire shotgun and again when the central-fire gun was adopted.

Opposite
Viewed from the rear you can see how the hammers have been altered so
that they still strike the caps but without the "hen toed" look!

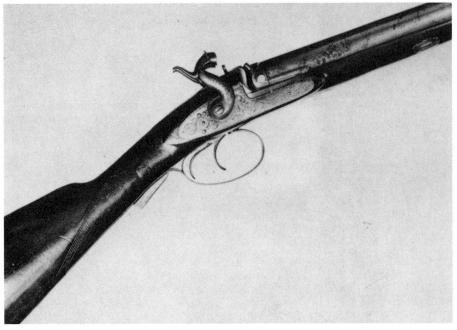

Double muzzle-loading shotgun, with grip safety, by John Dickson,
Edinburgh.

A STRANGER IN THE CAMP

As the years go by and one's store of knowledge increases there is a tendency towards complacency. One of the many fascinating aspects of having "an interest in firearms" is that every now and again this complacency is rudely shattered and, suitably humbled, there is a very real appreciation of the fact that no matter how much time has been devoted to study there remains a great deal to learn.

The weapons in my own modest collection are all familiar friends, I know their background and personal history and, if asked, I can spin a yarn about each one of them and answers to all questions are readily supplied. All, that is, except one, the "stranger in the camp". This is a good quality Dickson percussion muzzle loader, smooth-bore, about 14-bore. It has 30 in. twist barrels, which, if browned would show a good figure and, although the figure in the stock is not exceptional, the metal furniture is pleasingly engraved.

It has seen a good deal of service and was badly neglected when it came into my hands. I doubt if I would have bothered with it had it not been a Dickson, but, for personal reasons, I collect Dickson guns and for this reason it was brought home and given a superficial cleaning so that I could see what sort of bargain I had got.

The first thing that attracted attention was a narrow "plate" in the trigger guard

The small circular "trapdoor" or flap is seen here. The hinge of the flap
is attached to a small piece of metal inlet into the false breech.

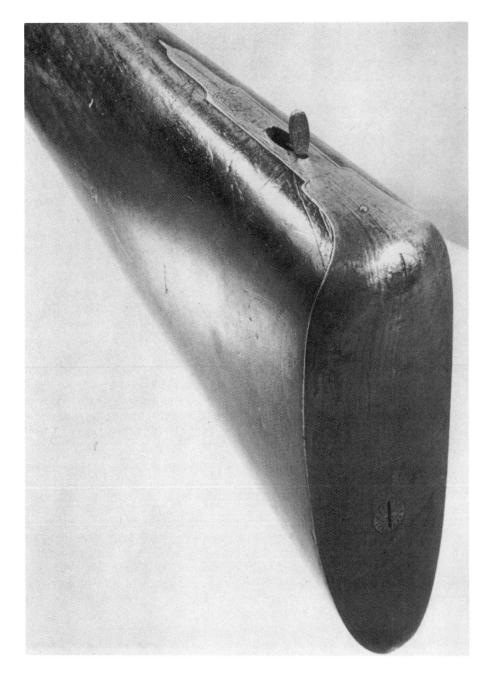

The other trapdoor or flap is oval instead of round and is to be found in the tang of the butt plate.

tang. When this was cleaned and freed it turned out to be the lever of a grip safety. Slightly unusual but not unique. Joseph Manton is usually accredited with the invention of the grip safety but there were many later modifications and improvements following the introduction of the percussion muzzle loader, and with the breechloader safety devices, particularly with "hammerless" actions, were a *sine qua non*.

In the years between 1855 and 1865 fourteen safety systems were patented. These could be broken down into several basic systems; one of which relied on the upward pressure of a lever in the trigger guard tang which was depressed when the small of the stock was grasped in the act of firing. An alternative was to have the lever on the top of the grip pressed by the right hand on firing.

The small spring-loaded lever on the Dickson was no mystery therefore. When in the down position it locks the triggers, whether the hammers are down at half cock or at full cock, and providing that it is kept in good order and not allowed to be gummed up, it works quite well.

This was not all, however; the Dickson had two further secrets which were revealed but not explained as cleaning progressed. On the top of the false breech was a small circular affair, in front of the head of the stock screw. This on further examination proved to be a small circular hinged plate or flap which could be lifted so that it stood vertically. The general appearance when raised can be seen in the photographs – it stands upright just in front of the cocked hammers, and when open there is a small hole underneath. What on earth was it for? Some sort of special sight or what?

I was still puzzling over this when the cleaning of the butt plate tang brought to light another little trapdoor, this time oval and spring loaded. What was the reason for this? Had the two little doors a separate function or were they part of something else, some device which has now been lost? The sight theory certainly doesn't fit the butt plate tang trapdoor. All sorts of ideas have been advanced to account for these little doors. None are convincing. There are no prizes offered for the solution, but I would welcome any suggestions as to their use.

CHARLES JONES PATENT LOCKS

In the article on "Ignition Systems" I promised to illustrate the Charles Jones Patent gun. I mentioned the rare and rather peculiar percussion caps which were used with the Jones gun. The caps are rare because few have survived and they are peculiar because the priming composition, instead of being inside the cap, is in a shallow depression on the outside of the cap. The specimen cap reached America from this country in a gun case and then came to me by a most complicated route through the kindness of Robert O. Cox of Fort Lauderdale.

The years went by until at a recent Game Fair who should arrive on the stand but Mr. R. MacLeod, and what did he have with him but a Charles Jones Patent shotgun no less!

If you look at the illustrations and compare this gun, which dates from about 1840, with conventional percussion muzzle-loading shotguns you will see a number of interesting and unusual features.

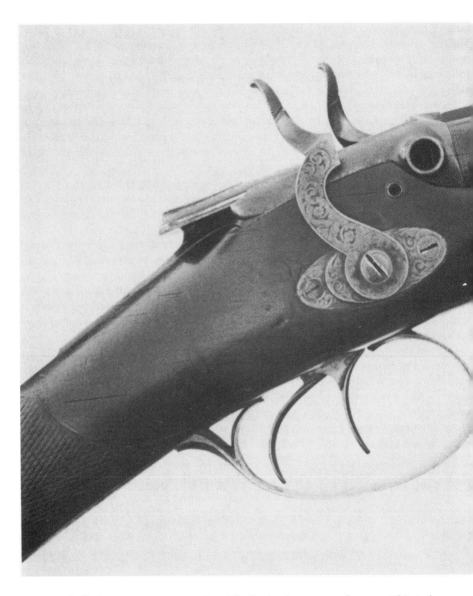

First of all there are no conventional locks in the accepted sense. This is because Charles Jones patented an internal percussion lock mechanism in 1833.

What appear to be external hammers are, in fact, cocking levers, to cock the internal firing mechanism. The strikers, for that is what we should call them, can be seen in the illustration taken from the top of the gun. A sliding plate has been opened and the two strikers can be seen, also the internal nipples which are screwed into the breech ends of the barrels. The hole you can see at the side of the gun is a vent for the escape of gas. If

As a muzzle-loading gun, the Jones is unusual, but not so unusual as to be considered eccentric. The small "lock plates" appear strange, as does the unusual shape of the cocking levers. That the gun is of high quality is evident from the shape of the triggers and trigger guard.

you imagine trying to place a conventional cap on to the nipple of the barrel I think you will agree that this would not be an easy task, and certainly not in the field in cold and wet conditions.

This is where Charles Jones displayed his inventive skill. It is difficult to put a cap on the nipple but far less difficult to place one over the nose of the striker. The only problem is that with the cap on the striker the priming is inside where it will do no good. The answer is simple. Put the priming on the outside of the cap so that the flame

With the sliding cover open the two hammers can be seen, one at full cock, the other in the fired position. Also the shape of the hammer nose is so designed to take the special externally primed cap. The corrosion on the front of the lid shows that the gun has seen quite a lot of use!

will be directed into the nipple and so ignite the charge in the barrel.

This is what Jones did and some of his strange caps have survived to this day. Contemporary literature tells us that the system was highly thought of and we can verify that at least this gun was used in this way because the firing mechanism shows signs of considerable use. This then was not merely an interesting toy, but a gun which was liked and well used.

It was not only the use of a cover that kept out the rain (hence the inscription on the gun – Charles Jones Patent Waterproof Locks), but also, possibly of even greater importance, was the fact that the system with its sliding cover protected the shooter's eyes against cap fragments, something which happened all too often with percussion cap guns.

Jones listed some fifteen advantages to his patent locks in an advert of 1835 and therefore it is hardly surprising that he was "Gun Maker to HRH Prince Albert".

Little is known about Jones because he was in business only from 1832 to 1845. He made guns and pistols at 16 Whittal Street, Birmingham, but also had a retail outlet in St James's Street, London. Charles Jones was in no doubt as to the effectiveness of his invention for he stated in his publicity that "there are a greater number of improvements effected, and more points of real usefulness attained in them, than have ever before been accomplished *at any one period* in the history of gun making". Looked at from the modern aspect of the Trades Descriptions Act the statement stands on the italicised phrase and one's interpretation of how long a "period" is.

It would be of the greatest interest to have comment on the system by a practical shooting man of the period. A search through the literature has so far drawn a blank, but somewhere I feel there is a useful note on Charles Jones' patent lock.

WILLIAM GREENER'S MUZZLE LOADER

If you look at the illustration overleaf where I have laid the gun across the pages of Greener's book you can see the restrained quality of the engraving. Note particularly the hammers. For want of a better term I think I will call these "Newcastle" hammers. I should have liked to have had a term ready which was a little more erudite. There are at least ten distinct types of percussion hammer; the ones fitted to this Greener are themselves typical of a very distinct style, and in honour of the birthplace of Greener I'll call this style "the Newcastle pattern". There are another nine to name but I'll leave that until another time. To show you the care and attention to detail that went into the building of this gun I have chosen to illustrate one part, the metal pipe which projects the tip of the stock where the ram rod enters; just look at and enjoy the sheer delight of this quite insignificant bit of metal, it's only $2\frac{1}{2}$ ins. long but I get pleasure from just looking at it.

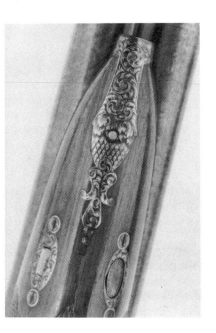

Attention to detail is one of many things which distinguish the quality gun from others. The detail, engraving and inletting of the ram-rod pipe speak for themselves!

William Greener's muzzle loader shown against the illustration of a similar though not identical gun in W. W. Greener's book, *The Gun and its Development.*

A LATE MUZZLE LOADER

One of the most amazing collections ever put together was that of Charles Gordon, and guns bought by him still appear or are shown to me by their puzzled owners.

Let us take the gun illustrated overleaf as an example. This is a truly splendid 12-bore percussion muzzle-loading shotgun by John Dickson of Edinburgh. Dicksons were the gunmakers who made all Charles Gordon's fantastic collection of new and

unused shotguns and rifles and the condition of the example illustrated is enough to alert the detective in me to the possibility that this could have been a Charles Gordon gun. A check on the number and, sure enough, this gun was bought by Gordon in 1889!

Although by this time I imagine that most people were using breechloaders and a few were purchasing new muzzle loaders it would be interesting to gain confirmation on this point. I can't imagine that Charles Gordon was the only man eccentric and wealthy enough to indulge his fancies for obsolete firearms by having them specially built for him. In an age when such behaviour was amusedly tolerated there must have

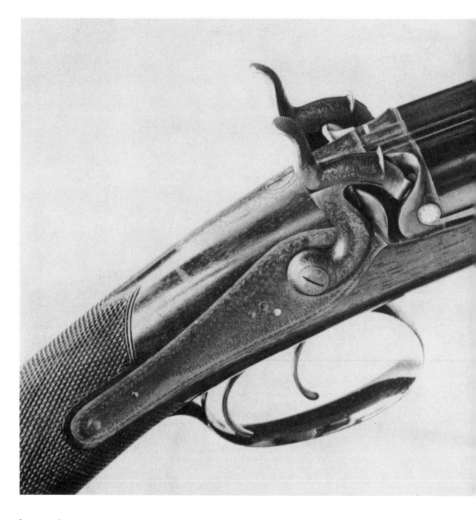

been other men with similar tastes. Given the opportunity I would have been one for a start!

Why Gordon had these splendid muzzle loaders made for him I cannot say, I'm only very glad that he did. This example shows gunmaking at perhaps its highest point. The gun is sober in appearance, browned damascus barrels still showing signs of the superb polish with which they were originally finished and the breech plugs are case hardened.

A slight concession to fashion is the thin platinum inlay just ahead of the false breech and, of course, the platinum plugs in the breech. In line with current taste – for breech loading hammer guns were still being made with back action locks – the locks have the mainspring behind the tumbler and so this part of the stock has a pleasant rounded appearance which is very satisfying. The inletting of the lock-plates is faultless and the engraving, very fine scroll, cannot be faulted.

The magnificent double 12 bore percussion muzzle loader, made for Charles Gordon in 1889 by John Dickson of Edinburgh.

The high standard of finish on the trigger guard is remarkable and even from the photograph some indication of the quality of the charcoal blueing can be gained. The stock is plain and without ornate figure but the quality of the chequering is high and whilst the pattern cannot be seen from the illustration it is unusual and effective.

This is a truly beautiful shotgun and, apart from slight pitting on the outside of the barrels, due no doubt to poor storage at one time or another, it must be in much the same condition as when it left the workroom of John Dickson over 80 years ago.

To me, the gun has that slightly odd look of things which are "out of period" rather like a 1983 replica of an SSK Mercedes Benz. It would be interesting to find out if I get the same feeling with similar "out of period" guns (assuming that they exist) when I don't know their history!

4

Shooting the
Muzzle-loading Shotgun

A modern muzzle-loading double shotgun by Pedersoli, ideal for shooting
today under modern conditions.

30 MIDLAND GUN COMPANY, Demon Gun Works, Bath Street, BIRMINGHAM, 4.

Muzzle-Loading Guns All Bores
Single Muzzle-Loading Guns OUR OWN MAKE

WHITE METAL VENT

WHITE METAL ROD

No. 3858
Regd. unbreakable Aluminium Ramrod, brass worm and tip.

No. 3858—Single barrel, superior quality bar action lock, steel barrel with rib, hardened lock plate, nicely engraved, blued furniture chequered walnut stock. Our Registered Metal Ramrod .. .. Price £2 0 0

**CAP BOXES
3/6 extra.**

WHITE METAL VENT

WHITE METAL ROD

No. 3870
Unbreakable Aluminium Ramrod, brass worm and tip.

No. 3861—Single barrel, patent breech with break-off, superior quality bar lock, steel barrel, with rib, hardened breech,break-off and lock plate, well-engraved, blued furniture, chequered walnut stock and fore-end. Our Registered Metal Ramrod .. .. Price, £2 10 0
No. 3870—Single Barred as No. 3861, but finer quality Engraving and finish (As Illustrated). .. .. .. Price, £3 0 0

Double Muzzle-Loading Guns

NOTE.—All our M.L. Guns fitted with our Registered unbreakable Aluminium Ramrod.

WHITE METAL VENT

WHITE METAL ROD

No. 3947—Double barrel, steel barrels, patent breech, with break-off, superior quality bar locks, hardened break-off and lock plates, neatly engraved, chequered walnut stock. Aluminium Ramrod, Brass worm and tip complete
Price £3 10 0

**DEMON QUALITY
MILITARY PERCUSSION CAPS.
Waterproof, 6/3 per 1,000.** | **SPORTING M.L. CAPS
4/6 per 1000
For Guns on this page.**

Spare Aluminium Ramrods, worm and tip complete, 2/- each.

WHITE METAL VENT

WHITE METAL ROD

No. 3965.
No. 3957—Double barrel, fine steel barrels, patent breech with break-off, superior quality bar locks, hardened breech break-off and lock plates, well finished, walnut stock, full chequered hand and fore-end, Aluminium Ramrod, brass tip and worm .. .. Price £3 15 0
No. 3965—Double barrel, as No. 3957, but superior quality Engraving and finish. Rolled shoulders (As Illustrated) Price £4 10 0

NOTE.—Above Guns are made in these Works and Guaranteed.

FOR CASES AND IMPLEMENTS SEE PAGES 11, 17, 50 to 52.

Shooting the muzzle-loading shotgun

As the interest in things of the past continues to grow it is not surprising that there is an ever increasing number of people who shoot, or would like to shoot, muzzle-loading shotguns. For the purposes of this chapter the term muzzle-loading means percussion muzzle-loading shotguns.

Although it is possible to persuade someone to lend you a gun it is better by far to have your own to learn how to obtain the best results. There are, of course, replicas as well as originals on the market. Although we may think that shooting with muzzle-loading, percussion shotguns is quite recent it has been going on continuously since Forsyth invented the detonating gun in the early part of the nineteenth century.

Somewhere or other a muzzle loader has been fired at quite regular intervals throughout the whole of the intervening period. Gunmakers have been making muzzle-loading guns continuously since then and, as some of the late ones do turn up and confuse us, it is best to start with an appraisal of the whole range likely to be encountered.

Let's look first of all at the typical muzzle-loading, percussion gun; lock, stock and barrel. The locks which are fitted to these guns have external hammers (with one or two very rare exceptions). If the gun is single barrelled then the lock will almost always be found on the right hand side of the stock.

Two types of lock are to be found, bar-action and back-action. In the bar-action lock the mainspring is in front of the hammer but with the back-action the mainspring lies behind the hammer. You can't see the mainspring with the locks attached to the stock but you can get a good idea where it is from the shape of the lock plate.

If you pull back the hammer you will find on most locks (the Rigby is one exception) that you come to the half cock position first of all and then to the full cock position. As you draw back the hammer (with your finger clear of the trigger) you can hear each click quite clearly (or you should be able to) and the trigger will give a little twitch. When on full cock, if you wish to lower the hammer, it must first be pulled back, held firmly, and the trigger pressed and then the hammer lowered, under restraint. It is obviously very good practice to do this always with the muzzle of the gun pointing in a safe direction, even when you know the gun is unloaded.

If you look closely at the nose of the hammer you will see that it is recessed and the shroud should be unbroken since this helps to prevent the bits of copper from the cap

Opposite
Yet another class of muzzle loader are those made in the first half of the twentieth century. These single and double guns were offered for sale by the Midland Gun Company in the 1920s and '30s. Few appear to have survived in the UK.

A good example of a sound, plainly finished muzzle loader probably made in Birmingham for the Scottish gunmaker Murray of Stonehaven late in the nineteenth century. Guns of this type continued to be made long after the introduction of the breechloader for use by game keepers and estate workers.

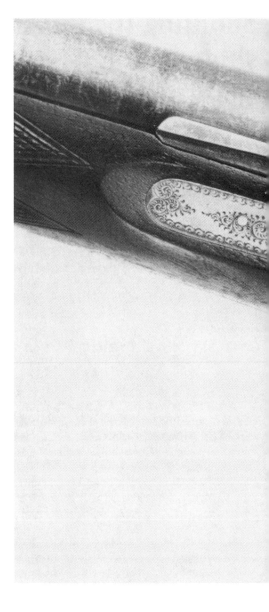

flying about and possibly causing injury to yourself or someone near to you.

The gun stock, into which the locks are let, differs from a breech-loading shotgun stock in that it is in one piece; the fore-end is attached to the butt stock and cannot be removed. The shape and style of the stock are not all that different from a modern double breechloader since the general styling of British shotgun stocks was laid down by Manton in the days of the flintlock and has remained essentially unchanged since

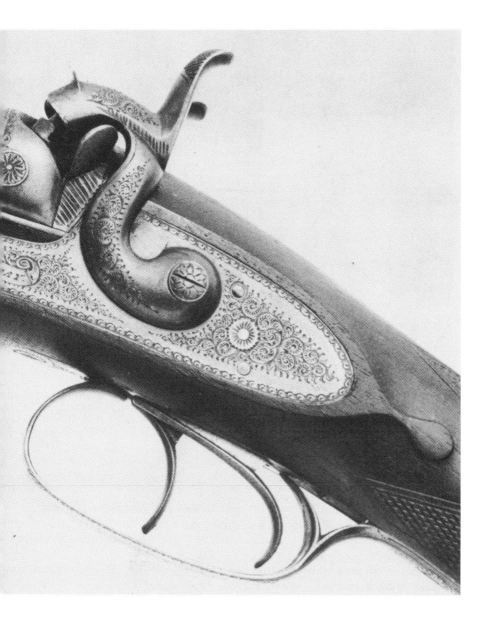

then. The stock should fit you, not too long and not too short. It is unlikely that it will be unduly cast off or on and you will find that in all probability the end of the stock is shod with a steel butt plate. This was often discarded by those who made breech-loaders but the steel butt plate of a muzzle-loading gun does serve a useful purpose. This can be clearly appreciated when you realise that when loading the gun, it has to be placed with the butt on the ground and the steel butt plate serves as a useful protection.

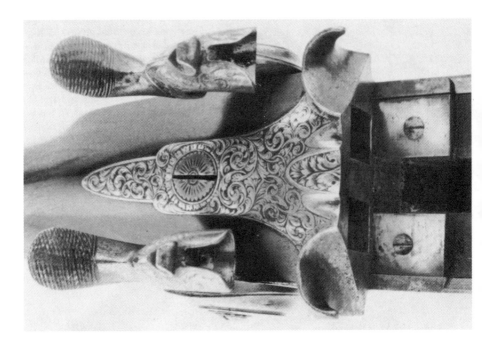

The cross bolt in the fore-end has been pushed clear of the barrel loops
and the barrels unhinged from the stock. Clearly seen are the two slots in
the false breech into which the barrels hook and the protective metal
plates let into the stock.

I

The stock can have a straight hand or a pistol hand as with modern guns but quite
often the muzzle loader is found with a scroll trigger guard which serves as a pistol
hand. The lockwork is simply let into the stock and below are the triggers with their
steel guard.

Attached to the stock above the locks is the false breech. This has two slots on the
face into which two hooks (in the case of a double shotgun) fit and secure the breech
end of the barrels. The barrels are held firmly in place by a cross-bolt passing through
the fore-end from left to right and holding the barrels by means of a "loop" attached to
the underside of the barrels. On guns of good quality the wood of the fore-end is
protected from damage by the cross-bolt by two small, oval, metal plates. Generally,
you cannot lose the cross-bolt since it is prevented from coming completely away from
the fore-end by means of a small pin. Don't try and push the bolt right out of the fore-
end otherwise the retaining pin will be damaged.

Now let's have a look at the barrels. If the gun is original and in good condition the

The breech end of the Greener barrels showing the hooks which fit into the slots in the false breech. The nipples used have two flat sides; others which you might encounter are four-sided and require a different type of nipple key. Some nipples are marked L and R; replace them in the left- and right-hand side barrels if removed.

first thing you will notice is that the barrels are brown and not black or blue. Also there will be a rather odd pattern on the barrels which can vary from a spiral of dark and light brown to a pattern of whorls rather like fingerprints. If properly cared for and correctly proofed, the barrels will stand the correct charge of black powder and shot.

The barrels have a top and bottom rib like modern ones but underneath you will find one or two small tubes. These are called ramrod pipes and, if you are fortunate, you will find a ramrod which passes through the two pipes into the "tail pipe" which protects the end of the fore-end where the ramrod enters the stock. The ramrod has one brass reinforced end which is used to press down the wads. The other end has a removable ferrule protecting a "worm" or small corkscrew, which is used to pull the charge if the gun has been loaded and is not to be fired.

If we put the locks to half cock, press out the cross-bolt and also remove the ramrod, the barrels can be unhooked from the standing breech. With them removed you will find the proof marks and an indication of the bore size of the barrels stamped underneath. If you look closely at the breech end of the barrels you will find that they are closed up. To the man changing from a muzzle loader to a breechloader all those years ago the fact that we shoot with barrels which are open at both ends would be somewhat surprising and perhaps slightly disquieting. The muzzle-loading shooter was used to having a solid breech plug screwed into the end of the barrel between him and the charge. The breech plugs can be seen since they are a different colour to the rest of the barrel and there is usually an obvious join. Both breech plugs can be removed by unscrewing. If you look closely you will see why this is. I do not recommend that you try and unscrew the plugs since they are fitted very tightly and you can damage the barrels if you do not take care. If for any reason the plugs have to be removed (to verify the internal state of the barrels for example) take them to a properly qualified gunsmith.

Into the breech plugs you will find little pegs screwed. These are hollow and are today known as nipples. In early books on shooting they are called "pegs" or "pivots". Beneath the nipples you will see the vent plugs usually of platinum if the gun is of good quality, and, sometimes, if you buy an old gun, they may well have been removed so is wise to check that they are still there.

Now that you know what to look for the next thing is to know where to look. There are a number of specialist firms who sell original muzzle-loading guns and also there are the various sale rooms and auction houses who specialise in this type of shotgun. How much you have to pay will obviously depend on the quality of the gun and its condition. You can buy a good quality gun, have any damage or wear made good and end up with a gun that is as good as new. Remember that muzzle loaders were still being made in this country until about 35 years ago and are still being made in Belgium, Spain and Italy. Today there are replica, muzzle-loading shotguns made for the enthusiast who uses one as his only gun or perhaps as a second gun so that his "best" original is not subjected to the strain of continuous use.

II

A replica muzzle-loading shotgun, more or less available off the shelf, can be bought for less than £150. This is the model L241 made by Pedersoli and imported by Parker-Hale, which is a double-barrelled 12-bore with 29½ in. barrels, an overall length of 45 in. and weighing about 5¾ lb. Incidentally, the light weight is one of the benefits of the muzzle-loader. The Pedersoli can be bought from several firms who stock muzzle-loading guns, such as the J.L.S. Arms Company of 28 Market Place, Wednesbury, West Midlands.

How can you get hold of an original British muzzle loader and what would you expect to pay for it? This is not an easy question to answer so I asked the people at Christie's. Desmond Healey, to whom I spoke, told me that a cased, percussion, muzzle-loading shotgun with all the usual accessories in good condition, and of good quality, would fetch about £500 to £650. A shotgun in medium to good condition, again of good quality but lacking case and tools, would be between £300 to £400 and a shootable gun by a minor maker could be bought for about £150 (1978).

Before you raise your eyebrows at these prices remember that at the top end of the market you will be competing with the chap who is buying as a collector or maybe as an investment and he does not intend to shoot the gun that you would so dearly love to have. A gun with evidence of honest wear and tear may not be as attractive to the collector and consequently the price could be lower. A gun with the name Purdey or Lancaster on the rib and locks will fetch more money than a gun of equal quality by a maker whose name is less well known, but which, as far as you are concerned, will shoot just as well. The price which you will have to pay is determined by many factors, some of which are to a large extent unpredictable. There are, however, a number of people who will be willing to help you find your gun but you will have to pay them for their trouble. It is when you decide to search for the gun yourself that problem areas can arise. The basic things to look for are undented and corrosion-free barrels which are also of adequate thickness and have not been polished down to the thickness of paper to remove the effects of past neglect. This you cannot check without the proper tools, but barrels, the muzzles of which could be used to sharpen pencils, must be looked at with more than just ordinary caution.

Beware of the "home gunsmith" who may have put one of his failures on the market to get rid of it, although it may be useful for spare parts. The barrels may have loose rust and this can be removed by repeated scrubbings with a wire brush, steel wool and oil such as "3-in-1". If there is any original finish use rough flannel and a lot of "elbow

A modern muzzle-loading double shotgun by Pedersoli, ideal for shooting
today under modern conditions.

grease". If the job is too much take it to a gunmaker who will give you his opinion and an estimate for doing the job.

It is essential to remove the nipples. If they are tight and, using the proper nipple key, they cannot be shifted then soak them in penetrating oil. Dip the whole breech end of the barrels in oil and fill them inside for a few inches as well and leave, if necessary, for several days. Sometimes damaged nipples can be rescued by using a fine file but often the only answer is replacement which may be required because of the non-availability of properly fitting caps. Check that the barrels are a tight fit to the stock. Looseness can be corrected by shimming the standing breech and a check on the cross-bolt and barrel loop may show where a slight adjustment can correct the looseness.

The breech plugs can be removed and under certain conditions their removal is well nigh essential. This is not a job for the beginner who will probably lack the proper tools and besides the distinct possibility of causing damage to the barrels, the ribs might spring loose.

If you are landed with a gun which has a hole in the barrel it might be worthwhile investigating the possibility of having the barrels re-tubed or sleeved. I don't know of anyone who has done this but I see no reason why the job cannot be done. The end result would mean that your muzzle loader would have steel barrels, which in itself may be no bad thing.

III

Next we come to the locks. On older guns these are held in place by one pin or screw passing through both lock plates. The head of the screw is to be found on the left hand lock plate. It may not be seen until the left hand lock is brought to full cock. Sometimes the other end of the screw also has a screwdriver slot. Always try the "screw" in the left hand lock plate and the one with the biggest head.

Talking about screwdriver slots it is absolutely essential that you either have or get hold of a full set of proper screwdrivers. If you do not have screwdrivers (or turn-screws) then don't even start tinkering with your gun. Tight screws will defeat you and you will damage and burr the screwdriver slots and make it more difficult for the chap who comes after you to clear up the mess. The screwdriver should be of the correct width to use the entire length of the slot and it should also fit the slot from side to side. Many screw slots have parallel sides and so a screwdriver with the tip correctly shaped is needed. Keep your set of screwdrivers for gunsmithing and don't let anyone else use them for other jobs.

Bear in mind that the locks have to be at least on half-cock to clear the nipples before they can be removed. With the locks off check the inside for rust and pitting. Check also for hardened oil. If you have to dismantle to clean them thoroughly then you will need a mainspring cramp. This can be made from a piece of metal and used for one lock but cramps with an adjustable screw can be bought and are better in the long run. Bring the lock to full cock, fit the cramp, release the hammer slowly and carefully disengage the swivel and ease the mainspring clear. The screws or pins securing the bridle are then taken out and the bridle removed. Remember to replace these pins in precisely the same holes you took them from. If you don't the operation of a fine lock can be compromised. "Three-in-one" oil, flannel and a good soaking should get off most of the rust and dirt. If you have to remove the tumbler then a bit more work is required and the hammer has to be taken off. This means removing the screw you will find in the middle of the hammer and, again, a good screwdriver is essential.

Always ensure that the part you are handling is properly supported and watch out for the small screws. The more important the screw the quicker it is lost, the more difficult it is to find, and the more inaccessible is the place where it got to. That's Boothroyd's First Law of Gunsmithing!

One other place which often needs attention is the trigger area. To get at the triggers means a bit more work with that "special" screwdriver. The two screws in the trigger guard tang have to be removed (one only if the stock has a pistol grip). Then the guard can be unscrewed by rotating the tang. The screw holding the front of the guard is attached to it and enters the front of the trigger plate. The trigger plate has two screws, one of which you can see even before the guard is removed, while the other is underneath the guard. With all these screws removed you may still find that the trigger plate cannot be shifted. This is because the screw passing through the standing breech tang also enters the trigger plate from above. This is a big, strong screw and needs a lot of shifting. Don't be upset by the effort needed to move the screws. Tight fitting screws are better than loose ones.

With the trigger plate removed make certain that all rust and caked-on oil is removed, the triggers are free and that the little springs are correctly operating as they keep the trigger blades in contact with the sear tails and stop rattling noises. It does mean, however, that when you replace the locks you will have to push the triggers forward before you can get the locks back. Closely examine each part when it is removed; see how it fits into place and how carefully it was made. Ensure that you do not damage parts and so create more havoc than you set out to remove. The locks and triggers are beautiful pieces of mechanism so treat them with respect and care.

Last of all have a look at the stock. Check it for cracks and also for past repairs that may not have been properly carried out. Some linseed oil rubbed into the wood will help clean and improve the appearance. I don't advise a costly refinish job at this stage. Later, we will look more closely at the other bits and pieces you will need to enjoy using a muzzle loader and how you can keep the gun in good condition. Finally we will deal with loading and shooting the gun and the safety precautions which must be observed.

IV

Your muzzle-loading shotgun is either a replica, new or possibly secondhand, or it is a mid-nineteenth century British-made gun which you have purchased in sound condition, ready for use. If you were not able to afford an "as new" gun then you have been working away stripping and cleaning a sound and serviceable gun and in

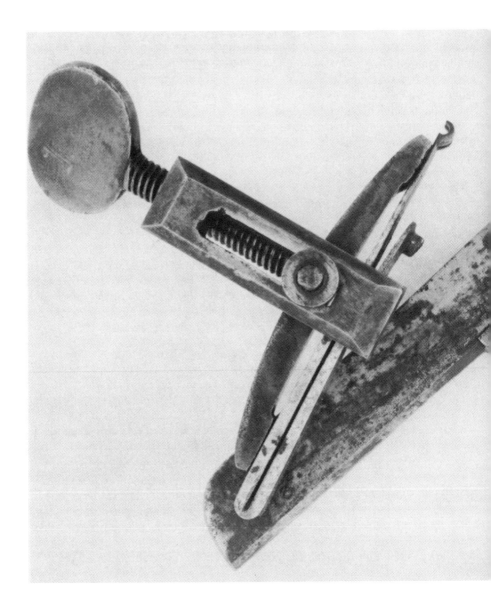

exchange for all that work you obtain a gun slightly more cheaply than you would have had it been in pristine condition. But, of more importance, you now know something of the mechanism and general construction of a muzzle-loading gun.

If you did have the gun in bits you will have seen the proof marks underneath the

Percussion lock (less hammer) with the mainspring cramped for removal. The screw cramp illustrated will sometimes be found in a gun case, but simple "C" cramps can be made and work well.

barrel and the figures which indicate the bore sizes. If they are not legible then you can measure the bore size roughly by using a Vernier scale on the muzzle diameter or taking the weapon to a gunshop for measurement.

As a guide the bore sizes and their decimal inch equivalents are:

10 g – 0.775	11 g – 0.751	12 g – 0.729
13 g – 0.710	14 g – 0.693	15 g – 0.677
16 g – 0.662	17 g – 0.649	18 g – 0.637
19 g – 0.626	20 g – 0.615	

If we take as an example the Greener that is marked 17. This is equivalent to 0.649 in. in diameter but the muzzle checks out at 0.665 in., slightly larger than a 16-bore. The difference is 0.016 in. which, for all practical purposes, can be disregarded. The answer is, of course, that the muzzle is relieved and the true bore size will be found lower down the barrel.

The bore size is of importance in order to determine two things. The size of the wadding that one has to use and the charge of powder and shot. The diameter of the wads is not critical since both the main wad and the overshot wad are made from compressible material. Card is the best wad for placing over the shot and card wads can be purchased or cut from cardboard with a wad punch. The cardboard should be stiff and it is advisable to make a small hole in the centre of the wad to let the air escape when the wad is rammed home on top of the shot. This is not so important in the case of the over powder wad since excess air can escape through the vent.

If you are fortunate in having a muzzle-loading gun of nominal 12- or 16-bore then

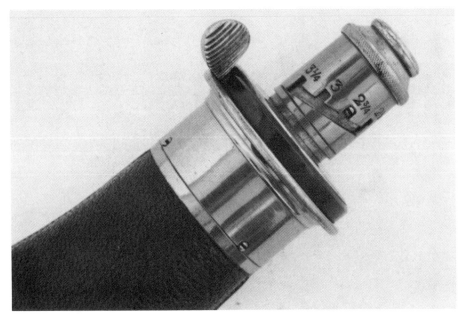

Close-up of the powder flask showing the outside spring top and the graduations on the measure from 2½ to 3¼ drams; the flask is set for 2¾ drams.

At the top right we have a tin of black powder. On top of this is a nipple key with pricker which screws into the top of the key. To the left a leather shot flask and to the right a shot belt with "inside charger", next to which is a tin of caps. Last of all we have the powder flask with a brass top, covered in Morocco leather.

you can buy suitable wads. If you have a gun with a more unusual bore size then you must make the wads yourself. Suitable punches can be obtained either from specialist suppliers or from a good ironmongers.

With a suitable supply of wads three more things are needed. Shot, powder and caps. Today we are rather more fortunate than the chap shooting in the first half of the nineteenth century. At least we know what size No. 6 shot is and how many we can expect to find in one ounce. Not so in days gone by. Shot sizes varied very widely dependent on the maker. In fact, by the mid-nineteenth century No. 6 shot varied from 326 to as little as 219 pellets to the ounce. Today, in this country one ounce of No. 6 shot contains 270 pellets. This information is given as a caution in the event of shotgun performance of a century ago being discussed. It is important to find out whether "London" or "Bristol" shot was being used.

Modern shot is of uniformly good quality but if bought loose it should be checked. I used to use shot taken from the old hollow brass counterweights which one found on early electric lights. This shot was by no means consistent, nor indeed was it round! Muzzle-loading guns are proofed with black powder and it is important that this type of powder is used and not modern smokeless powders. I have seen more than one splendid muzzle loader blown up by emptying a modern shotgun cartridge and putting the powder, wads and shot into the barrel of a percussion gun.

One instance was where the owner had run out of black powder and emptied the contents of a 16-bore cartridge into his 16-bore percussion s.b. shotgun. The gun was fired and the owner woke up in hospital. He still carries a piece of the barrel in his wrist.

V

The quality of black powder depends on the purity of its three ingredients – nitre, sulphur and charcoal and is greatly influenced by the type of wood employed to make the charcoal. Black powder of high quality is still being made in certain parts of the world and I recommend that you buy yours and do not make it yourself.

Two systems of denoting the size of the powder granules are in use. The British system is merely a series of numbers from 2 to 8. The smaller the number the finer the grain. Today the range is much reduced; normally available are numbers 2 and 6. The number may be prefaced by the letters T.S. This merely denotes Treble Strong (an early puff for powder roughly equal to the phrase "whiter than white").

The other system used is the American where the letters FG are employed. FG is the coarsest grain and FFFFG the finest grain or smallest grain size. The four F powder is used for priming flintlocks. Triple F is for single shot pistols and percussion revolvers and double F is for rifles and medium bore shotguns. In Britain the F series powders are also used in the finer grain sizes but you will not find a G or g in the description. Very coarse grain powder, Colonel Hawker's or Captain Latour's powder, was available for duck and punt guns.

The most important things about black powder are to keep it dry so that it will behave properly as a propellant and ensure that it is kept well away from fire and sparks. Ignition of black powder, particularly fine powder dust, is very much easier than is the case with the later smokeless powders. It does not do to shake the powder, particularly in a metal container, and it should be used and stored with great care.

Lastly we come to the percussion caps. Again, these were once available in the greatest profusion but today the number of sizes available is greatly reduced, also the range of qualities. Like shot and powder there were a number of manufacturers of caps and each had their own system of numbering the caps in order to describe the quality and to indicate the cap diameter and length. Eley, Joyce and Kynoch each had a separate series of numbers, consisting of two digits, to describe size. The sizes available now are 12, 26 and 16S. The internal diameter of the cap is 0.180 in., 0.185 in. and 0.225 in. respectively. The No. 12 and 26 caps are of the same length, 0.232 in. and the 16S is 0.255 in. The E.B. Military cap (E.B. being Eley Brothers) is different in that it has a flange from which comes its popular name the "Top Hat" cap. The size of this cap is 0.228 in. diameter and 0.245 in. nominal length. This is the cap used for British military muzzle-loading rifles such as the Enfield.

As well as the shot, powder, wads and caps you also need some tools and odd bits and pieces. A powder flask is useful but not essential. These can be bought as antiques but replicas are also available. You can use the canister in which you bought the powder and measure from this into a powder measure. Otherwise you can make a powder measure from any suitable container. One such container in use many years ago was a clay pipe, the bowl of which held just the right charge of powder. Powder charges are usually described by weights. But for all practical purposes you will employ a volume measure. The powder measure, whether on a powder flask or a separate tool, will be calibrated in drams. Each dram is equivalent to 27.34 grains so that the standard 3 dram powder charge for a 12-bore is 82 grains by weight.

Shot is measured by weight in ounces and fractions of an ounce but again, for practical purposes, it is measured by volume. For convenience a shot flask is employed but one can be lucky and get a shot belt with the appropriate charger. All is not lost, however, if neither of these items is available. A suitable separate measure can easily be made. As an alternative to shot flasks, shot charges can be employed. If the originals are unobtainable then the small plastic containers now common can be used instead. These containers can also be used for powder. Sufficient will have to be carried for a day's shooting and the container can be reloaded at home with the home made measures or standard flask measures. A useful device is the cap dispenser. These are not easy to make but I have seen them advertised from time to time. Of great importance is a well fitting nipple key with pricker. If available without pricker then a piece of stiff wire can be employed. This is usually wound round a button of your shooting waistcoat. This garment is most useful since the pockets can hold caps and wads and provide enough pockets so that all the flasks, tools and gadgets can be disposed about the person in order to be easily and quickly available.

I assume that the ramrod or loading stick has a "worm" so that the charge can be withdrawn if required. A pair of shooting glasses are important when shooting breechloading weapons but they are vital when shooting muzzle loaders.

Now to a more serious note. Strange though it may seem you require more permits to shoot with muzzle-loading weapons than you do with modern breechloaders. That is in this country. Regardless of the age of your muzzle-loading shotgun, if you intend to use it for shooting it becomes a firearm by definition and therefore you require a shotgun certificate. Also, since your m.l. shotgun will be using black powder as the propellant you will need a licence to acquire gunpowder under the Control of Explosives Order of 1953. Both are to be obtained from your local police. Incidentally, if you wish to use a muzzle-loading rifle or pistol then you will need a valid firearm certificate to "purchase, acquire or possess"! It can be over a hundred years old, it can be regarded as an antique, but if you intend to use it then it becomes a firearm since,

A most useful accessory is the cap dispenser. Caps are so small that in cold weather they are difficult to handle in the field. Cap dispensers were made in various styles and are now available as replicas for those who cannot find an original.

apart from the time taken to load it, it is as effective a weapon as a modern breechloader – so be warned!

VI

Finally we come to the actual shooting of the muzzle loader. I assume that you have a sound gun (either an original or a replica), supplies of powder and shot and the

necessary tools and implements. One thing which we have not discussed so far is the load for your gun. More so than with breechloaders, the load for a muzzle loader employing black powder is subject to personal variations and allows full reign for the experimenter. However, as a guide these are the recommended loads:

Bore Size	10	12/13	14/15	16/17/18	19/20/21	22/30
Shot ozs	$1\frac{1}{2}$	$1\frac{1}{4}$	$1\frac{1}{8}$	1	$\frac{7}{8}$	$\frac{3}{4}$
Powder drms	4	$3\frac{1}{4}$	3	$2\frac{3}{4}$	$2\frac{1}{2}$	2

With your shot flask and powder flask regulated to throw the correct charges of powder and shot you can now load your shotgun. The first thing to do is to check that it is unloaded! Do this with the ramrod or loading stick. You check that the end of the rod enters the breeching and this can be simply gauged against the barrel length. Then place a cap on the nipple and holding the gun so that the muzzles point in a safe direction snap off the cap and check that the vent is clear.

With the butt of the gun placed on the toe of your boot (to protect the butt from mud etc.) and holding the barrels away from the body, charge each barrel with the correct amount of powder. Here I would advise the use of a separate measure. This ensures that the powder in the flask cannot be exploded by the charge being fired due to a spark in the barrel. With the powder loaded, place an over powder wad in each muzzle and press firmly home with the ramrod until the wad is firmly seated on the powder. It is advisable to leave the fired caps on the nipples, with the hammers in the down position during loading. Then charge with shot and make certain that only one charge of shot goes in each barrel; do not double charge either powder or shot. Then place a card wad in the muzzle and drive home on top of the shot with the ramrod or loading stick.

Never use the palm of the hand to press home the charge, always use the fingers and thumb. If the charge does explode for any reason the ramrod will merely fly out of the hand instead of passing through the palm of the hand. With the charge loaded hold the shotgun with the barrels pointed safely upwards and place the hammers at half cock. Remove the fired caps and re-cap.

Bring the hammer back to full cock on the barrel you intend to fire first and then fire the second barrel. Do not keep firing the right hand barrel without discharging the left barrel or the shot charge will tend to move with the continued recoil. In the event of a misfire bring the hammer to half cock, ensuring that the barrels are pointing in a safe direction. Remove the fired or defective cap and clear the vent of the nipple with the pricker. Re-cap and fire again. If the gun still does not fire observe the same precautions but remove the nipple and prime the breech end of the barrel checking that the nipple vent is clear before replacing and re-capping. Even if you have missed the powder charge enough can be introduced through the vent with the nipple removed to get the wads and shot out of the barrel. If the charge has to be removed then use the worm at the end of the ramrod but ensure that the caps have been removed from the nipples and see that the barrels do not present a hazard.

At the end of the day remove the barrels and unscrew the nipples. Place the barrels breech downwards in a plastic bucket with water and using a tight fitting swab "pump" water up and down inside the barrels until clean water emerges. Wash out with warm water to help dry out the barrels and oil with "Young's Cleaner" or a similar product. Clean the nipples in water and wipe over the hammers and locks to remove fouling. Oil carefully. It is prudent to check the condition of the gun again after a few days.

Muzzle-loading shooting with a shotgun is great fun. It is better to shoot by one's self or with a group of other muzzle loaders. Don't mix breechloaders and muzzle loaders if at all possible since there is a very distinct possibility that the breechloaders will get a bit impatient with the muzzle loaders and the latter, pressed to move faster than they should, may make mistakes.

Muzzle loaders are potentially more hazardous than breechloaders, and, consequently even more care must be taken to avoid accidents, which don't just happen; they are caused by haste, error and confusion. Haste is one of the major causes of problems and if you are using a muzzle loader for game shooting it might be better to use two and a loader!

5
The
Early Breechloaders

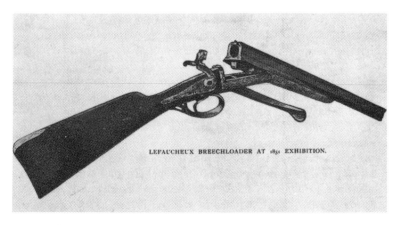

LEFAUCHEUX BREECHLOADER AT 1851 EXHIBITION.

The Lefaucheux gun shown at the 1851 Great Exhibition. The illustration is from the *Illustrated London News*.

The early breechloaders

THE PINFIRE

Not all that long ago, even a quite keen shotgun enthusiast, when confronted by a pinfire shotgun would say "It's only a pinfire, they all look alike to me". To many gunmakers the pinfire was just a nuisance, taking up valuable space, unsaleable and unusable. The apprentice was often put to work removing the stocks which were used to stoke the workshop cast iron stove, and the metal components were placed on the anvil and smashed up into smaller pieces for disposal as scrap.

Two factors determined my course of action regarding pinfires. The first was an acute lack of capital and pinfires were cheap, half a dozen tied up with binder twine for 5 shillings. The second was a belated realisation that they were an endangered species!

My interest was further stimulated when I realised that they were not all alike. Not only did the styling vary but also the mechanical details and once I found out that they could be returned to service and used, interest in pinfires became, for a time, even greater than that in muzzle loaders. Pinfires were of interest in that they had a gadgetry all of their own, cappers and de-cappers, extractors, in fact, a whole range of quite fascinating tools.

Today the pinfire has been the subject of quite serious study by a few dedicated enthusiasts. What has been exposed are quite serious gaps in our knowledge of the introduction of the breechloader into this country. Firearms where the propellant and projectile were loaded into the back or breech end of the barrel are almost as old as firearms themselves. What was different about the mid-nineteenth century breechloader was that the means of ignition was loaded as well, it was internal, part of the cartridge.

So, inescapably entwined with the development of the breechloader was the development of a self-contained cartridge. This is a complex subject in its own right, made even more difficult due to the absence of specimens of many of the early cartridges. For this, and other reasons, cartridge development will be dealt with separately, later in the book.

What has to be remembered is that the pinfire was not the first of the nineteenth century breechloaders with primer, powder and propellant loaded in "one package". Today we acknowledge that the Pauly was the first breechloader to fire a self-contained reloadable cartridge. The inventor was not British, not French but Swiss, Samuel Johannes Pauly and he became established in Paris shortly after 1800.

The Pauly appeared just five years after Forsyth's British patent of 1807 and it had a fixed barrel and an upwards hinged breech block pivoted on trunnions at either side of the barrel(s). It was to father a number of similar guns and ensured that the French remained of the opinion that having the barrels of their shotguns fixed and not hinged was an entirely sound idea! By comparison very few British shotguns were built with fixed barrels.

Pauly's central-fire breechloader with the hinged breech open to admit
the cartridges.

Since Forsyth's patent did not protect his invention in France, Pauly was able to
ɔtain percussion compounds to ignite his cartridge from the Parisian gunmaker
elat. Muzzle-loading guns with external percussion ignition were widely used by the
ench but the wealth of invention appears to have been directed to the breechloader.
gun similar to the Pauly appeared in 1831, the Robert. A hinged, lift up breech bolt
as again employed but on the Robert lifting the breech block with the long lever also
cked the locks. Another variation of the self-contained breechloading cartridge was
ed, this time with a small "tail" which contained the means of ignition. The
rtridge was unsatisfactory and, although the Robert appears to have enjoyed some
easure of success, it was short lived.

The man who had the greatest influence on the development of the sporting shotgun
as undoubtedly Casimir Lefaucheux, who, in the 1830s, took out a whole series of
tents covering breechloaders with hinged, downward pivoting barrels. The early
amples had external ignition but in 1836 Lefaucheux patented his pinfire cartridge
hich continued to be manufactured well into the twentieth century.

The system was, for a short time, used in Britain. The pinfire cartridge continued to

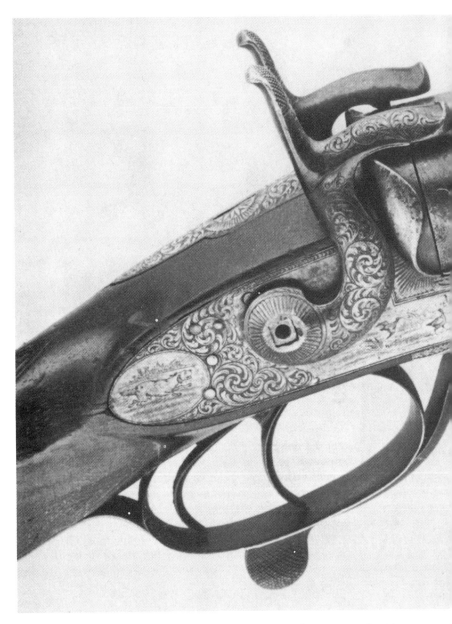

be manufactured in Britain and the Eley "Brown" pinfire in 12- and 16-bore was s•
listed in the I.C.I. Limited catalogue of 1935.

A simple view of the nineteenth century would be that flint ignition was replaced
percussion, following the Forsyth patent of 1807, and that percussion muzzle load·
were rendered obsolete by the Lefaucheux pinfire breechloader which was first seen

The distinctive pattern of the damascus barrels can be seen to advantage on the double pinfire by Marks. The style of engraving on the lock plate, large scroll and game scenes was to be almost standard on British sporting shotguns.

he Great Exhibition of 1851. The pinfire, in its turn, was then replaced by the central-ire shotgun and the remainder of the development was concerned with mechanical etail such as extractors, ejectors and self-cocking actions

A closer look reveals the gaps and inconsistencies mentioned earlier. How was it hat so little appears to have been known about the French breechloaders? Little was

written about them and that which was published was, in general, condemnatory
Peter Hawker, that most remarkable of sportsmen, was born in 1786 and he died in
1853. Widely travelled, inquisitive, opinionated and staunchly conservative in his
outlook, it was not until 1844 that he wholeheartedly accepted the percussion system
so his views on the French breechloader can be quite easily guessed.

> Let me caution the whole world against using firearms that are opened and loaded
> at the breech – a horrid ancient invention, revived by foreign makers, that is
> dangerous in the extreme.

Hawker goes on to say that he had seen and condemned a breechloader when he was in
Paris in 1841 and that in 1844 "he had heard of a man being killed by the very gun he
had seen".

J. H. Walsh, writing as was the fashion under a nom de plume, "Stonehenge"
admitted in *The Shotgun and Sporting Rifle* published in 1859 that there were "two or
three defects in the muzzle loader". He then goes on to say that the Lefaucheux or
"French Crutch Gun" (that name is damning in itself!) had been commonly used in
France for about twenty years before it was exhibited at the Great Exhibition in 1851
Before then "it was almost unknown in England".

Breechloaders must have been bought by visitors to Paris and brought back with
them to this country, even if only as a curiosity. Nearly two hundred years earlier the
famous diarist Samuel Pepys displays the sense of curiosity that cannot just have
atrophied by the early nineteenth century when he tells us about having seen (3 July
1622) "a gun to discharge seven times, the best of all devices I ever saw, and very
serviceable, and not a bauble, for it is much approved of and many thereof made'
Two years later his interest had not abated since he records "by coach to my Lord
Sandwich, with whom I spoke. ... There were several people by, trying a new fashion
gun ... to shoot often, one after another, without trouble or danger, very pretty."

Oh! for a nineteenth century sporting Pepys. Hawker, who should have told us
about developments in France is merely critical, and others, who saw guns and bought
them to bring home either recorded nothing, or if they did, what was written has been
lost.

The pinfire cartridge and the Lefaucheux had their defects and the British
gunmaker, once roused out of his apathy or complacency, set about improving the gun
and cartridge. One or two other systems enjoyed brief popularity and these are dealt
with in this section, along with the development of the breechloading pinfire.

The pinfire breechloader can be regarded almost as the Cinderella of the early
breechloading actions. Pinfire double shotguns are still to be found, rusty and
neglected with bores rather like the inside of a long disused sewer. The reign of the
pinfire was relatively short in Britain but it did herald the widespread adoption of the
breechloading system, although it was to be ousted by the central-fire.

Legend has it that the French Lefaucheux was introduced to Britain by Lang, then of
Cockspur Street, London. Initially, the shooting qualities of the pinfire were held to be
inferior to those of the muzzle loader and this feeling was borne out by a practical test
or trial of shotguns held in 1858. The standard load for a 12-bore in those days was a

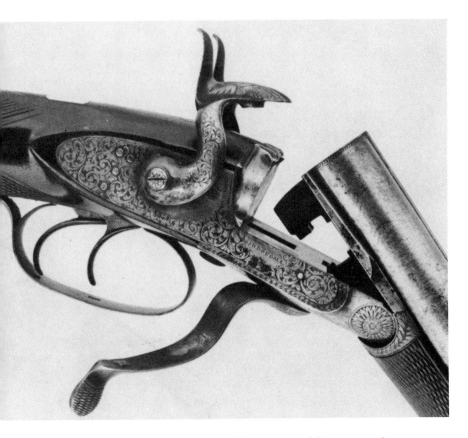

J. D. Dougall of Glasgow and London was one of the most vocal
protagonists of the pinfire system. This is a fairly typical example of the
British pinfire with bar action lockwork and double grip closure.

drams of black powder and 1¼ oz of shot. The first three places in the trial were taken
by muzzle loaders but they were hard pressed as regards both pattern and penetration
by the breechloaders. As far as speed of loading was concerned the breechloaders won
hands down and the initial disparity of performance was overlooked in favour of
increased convenience.

A further point against the original Lefaucheux action was lack of strength, the
barrels being bolted by a single hook engaging a slot or bite in the lump. There were
many alternative breech systems proposed and manufactured but by far the greater
number of pinfire guns were to employ the double grip action, as it was known in this
country, or the "English" or "T" action abroad.

Overleaf

A 14 bore pinfire double shotgun by Lyell of Aberdeen. Note the bar
action locks and pistol grip or "hand" on the stock.

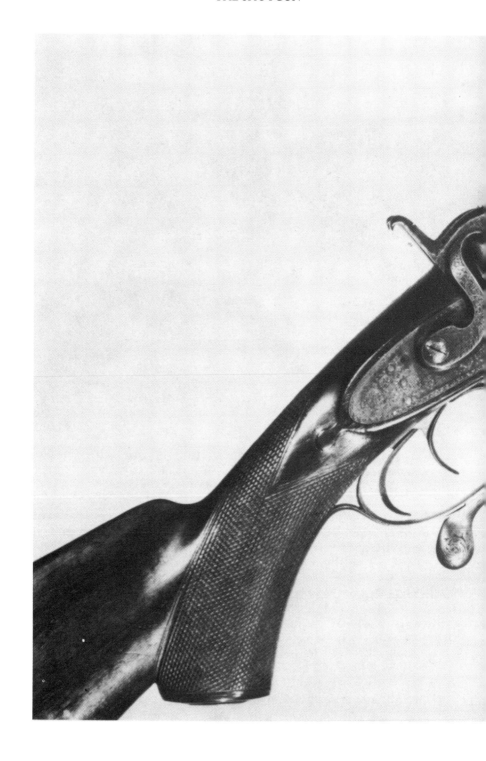

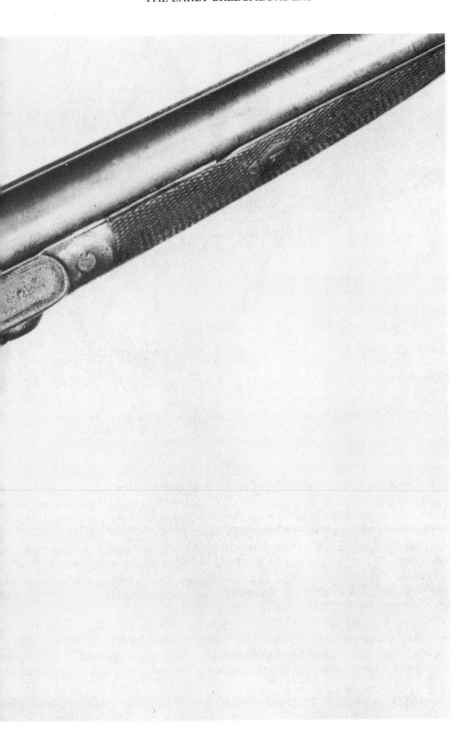

John Dickson broke away from the established pattern of the pinfire by
the use of a heavier style of underlever and square back trigger guard.
This example was made in 1863.

The double grip rotary underlever, with the lever extending back over the trigger
guard was convenient to use – far better, in fact, than the original Lefaucheux, where
the lever extended underneath the fore-end. In addition, the rotary bolt was arranged
so that it would partially snap although slight manual pressure was required to
complete the fastening. This bolt system long survived the pinfire shotgun and was
used extensively on all calibres of shotguns and large bore double rifles. It is, even
today, one of the strongest breech closures ever invented for hinge barrel actions and,
with practice, is not as clumsy in operation as perhaps first experience might have one
believe.

The major weakness of the pinfire shotgun lay with the cartridge. There was the
fear, slight though it may have been, that an accidental explosion could take place if
the cartridges were carried loose in the pocket. A more real problem existed in the
wear which took place in the channel or groove in the breech end of the barrel in which
the pin lay.

The use of reloaded cartridges, coupled with wear in the barrel channel, resulted in
gas escape and, on occasions, the pin could be blown out of the cartridge. The pin

could also become bent, in which case there was the likelihood of a misfire.

One major benefit of the pinfire was the lower cost as compared with the earlier central fire cartridges and guns. The chief competitor was the Lancaster central fire gun, the use of which was restricted by the higher cost. Four pinfire shotguns are illustrated. The first on pages 134 and 135 is by Marks of Winchester; 30 in. damascus barrels are fitted to this gun, a 12-bore, with London Proof. This gun has seen some hard wear and abuse but it is of good quality. The second gun illustrated on page 137 is by J. D. Dougall of Glasgow, a noted protagonist of the pinfire system. Perhaps not quite as nice a gun as the Marks but in better condition. The quality of the 29 in. damascus barrels is slightly inferior to the Marks. A minor point of difference is that the underlever is retained by a slot in the trigger guard into which a small lug on the inside of the lever fits. The Marks gun employs the more usual raised edge to the guard. Third in the series on pages 138 and 139 was made by John Lyell of Aberdeen. The most noticeable feature of this gun is the design of the hammers. Barrels are of best damascus 30 in. long, and London proofed. The Lyell gun is of very good quality and there is a full pistol hand with a horn cap. Last of all we have another double 12-bore (opposite), this time by John Dickson of Edinburgh and here the major difference is in the shape of the trigger guard and finger lever. Barrels are again 30 in. in length of good quality damascus.

All four pinfire guns are fitted with bar-action sidelocks, rotary underlever actions, cross-pin attachment of the fore-end and are remarkably similar in their appearance unless closely examined. This then was the "standard" pinfire gun of the mid-nineteenth century. Pinfire guns were fitted with back-action locks and there were many "patent" actions such as the Dougall "Lock Fast", Powell's patent snap action and those with a fixed breech and sliding barrels. Many enjoyed contemporary popularity but none were made in the same quantity as were those which employed the rotary underlever. If you have an old pinfire gun hidden away, rescue it from corruption by "moth and rust"; far be it for me to suggest that you return it to use, but at least preserve it for a little longer – the fault in the system lay with the cartridge, not with the gun.

6
Lefaucheux

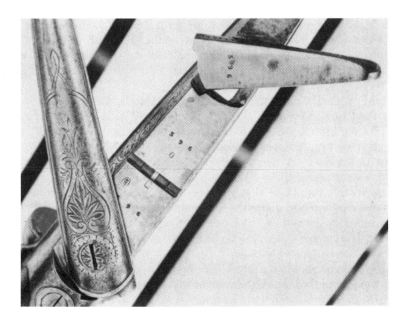

The Lefaucheux style of fore-end. The large lever opens the gun and the smaller lever at the tip of the fore-end holds the barrels in place. The levers can be all metal, horn or wood-covered.

Lefaucheux

Queries continue to be received concerning "The Lefaucheux Action". Since it is now some time since I last wrote about guns made on this design a review of what we know about the firm would not go amiss.

Lefaucheux is one of those people whose importance seems to have increased with the passing of the years rather than diminished. Where and when he was born is unknown to me. His given name was Casimir and he was the inheritor of the accumulation of inventive talents that had characterised French gunmaking in the second quarter of the nineteenth century. Paris was the centre of this group of people but the mainspring was not a Parisian, nor indeed a Frenchman, but a Swiss artilleryman who had served with the Army of Napoleon.

Samuel Johannes Pauly was a man of considerable inventive genius, and his gun, which he patented in France in 1812, was a breechloader. Unusual in this country but quite common in France, the Pauly gun had fixed barrels and a breech which pivoted upwards. His later pistols had a fixed breech and barrels which pivoted downwards. Pauly moved to London in 1814 and his Paris business was carried on by Henri Roux. M. Roux made certain modifications to the Pauly design and he, and his successor, M. Eugene Pichereau, continued to make and sell guns on the basic Pauly principle. Oddly enough the French source material ignores completely the work of Forsyth in the development of percussion ignition, illustrating one of the problems of the firearms historian!

It is at this point that Lefaucheux comes on the scene as "successor to M. Pichereau". The Pauly gun evolved into the "Fusil Robert" which employed a fixed barrel and pivoting breech and which, unlike the Pauly, was "hammerless". Some three years later, in 1834, Lefaucheux patented his gun.

This was a breakaway from current French thinking in that the barrels were hinged and dropped down. Beneath the barrels was what we today call "a lump" which has two opposing "bites". Into these bites a turning bolt locked, the bolt operated by a short lever which lay forward under the fore-end. This lever had a "handle" which fitted into a recess in the fore-end. I have never seen a Lefaucheux gun on these principles but oddly enough at the 1978 Game Fair I was able to see a Wiggan & Elliot pinfire gun with similar type of lever.

The later Lefaucheux guns had a metal fore-end and a curved metal lever under the barrel(s). By the time of the Great Exhibition of 1851 at which Lefaucheux, of 37 Rue Vivienne, Paris, exhibited, his shotgun looked very similar to those we know today. Back-action locks, external hammer with a large head, a now perfected pinfire cartridge and a long lever under the fore-end.

An example of this type of Lefaucheux is the pinfire double gun sold by James Bryce of Edinburgh. This gun was not made by Bryce but by Auguste Francotte of Liège. Francotte was one of the largest of the Liège arms manufacturers and the firm exported guns all over the world. This gun has the double bite locking but is quite plain although

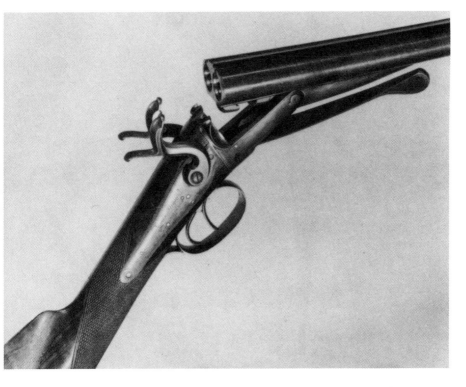

Liège-made pinfire with back action locks and "Lefaucheux" lever. The
Belgians referred to the lever under the fore-end as the "French lever".
This well-made gun was sold by Bryce of Edinburgh.

extremely well made. The fore-end is metal and on this example attached to the barrels
by a single screw. Similar in design is a far more ornate pinfire made in 1865 and
exhibited at the 1867 Paris World Fair.

A later variation has a larger lever but under this is a smaller lever which moves to
the left to remove the fore-end. This example is central-fire and is not dissimilar to the
later example shown with a wooden lever opening to the right and a horn shorter lever
for the fore-end. This gun has the metal fore-end and the double bite grip. The type of
action will be found in both pin and central-fire. The French would call this
"Fermeture à T, système Lefaucheux".

One other system which appeared in France was the Beringer, in which the lever is

Overleaf
The more exotic style of Lefaucheux-type pinfires were made in Liège.
This example was made in 1865 and was exhibited at the 1867 Paris
World Fair. (Musée d'Armes, Liège. 4719)

Illustrations of the early French Lefaucheux
shotguns show the lever along the fore-end but there
is a "cut-out" to take the enlarged end of the lever.
The sole example I have seen of this style (in a
slightly modified form) is this gun by Wiggan &
Elliot.

reversed and placed around the trigger guard or the lever is the trigger guard. Guns on
this pattern were made with both double bites, "fermeture à T", and a single bite, as
was the Lefaucheux.

When the "Lefaucheux" was made in this country the lever tended to be made
smaller and lighter and the metal fore-end of the French design was replaced by a
wooden one with the simple cross-bolt fixing which the British gunmaker had used on
the muzzle loader. Most had a simple lump brazed in between the barrels, the front end
of which bore against the hinge pin and at the rear was a single bite or notch. Unlike
the original Lefaucheux, the single bite was mechanically unsound whether used with
the forward facing Lefaucheux lever or the rear facing Beringer-type lever. Who first
turned the Lefaucheux lever to the rear and wrapped it around the trigger guard I
cannot say.

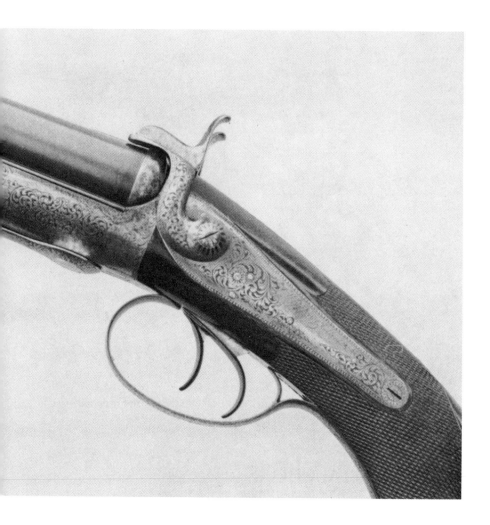

In Germany the lever guard and double bite is known as the "Englischer 'T' Doppelgriff" and in 1859 it was referred to in the British literature as the "back actioned lever". We, today, might call it the "Jones" action which was patented in 1859. One could simplify things and refer to the "fore-end lever" and the "guard lever" and to the single and double grip or "bite" locking. If names have to be given the term Lefaucheux would describe a pin or central-fire gun or rifle, with a forward lever lying under the fore-end either of metal, wood or horn and a metal fore-end attached by a single screw, a catch or lever. The barrel-locking could be either single or double grip.

Guns of this type had but a brief period of popularity in this country but were made and sold in France until the Great War and pinfire cartridges continued to be made until long after.

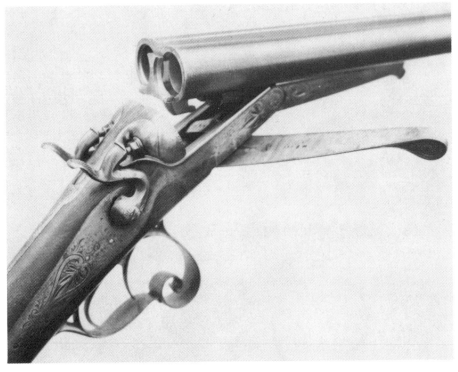

The Lefaucheux type of action lasted well into the centre-fire period.
This double gun by A. Evreux has a partial "snap action".

MODIFIED LEFAUCHEUX

When writing about old guns it is often very useful to have used them for the purpose for which they were originally intended. This is not always possible. Either the situation doesn't lend itself to firing off guns, or the gun is in such a condition that firing it would be imprudent – to say the least!

However, it is often possible to draw reasonable conclusions from experience of a similar type of weapon. My main experiences with the French Lefaucheux have been obtained from the use of a John Dickson central-fire Lefaucheux-type double 12. The reason why this gun was built has always eluded me – recourse to the records proved abortive – and using it with black powder cartridges brought sharply into focus one of the disadvantages of the Lefaucheux action.

As you can see from the illustration the lever which opens the gun lies along the fore-end and has to be pushed across to the right by the left hand. I don't know what technique the French sportsman used with this type of gun but I found that using the left hand to push the lever across I then laid the fore-end across my left forearm which allowed me to remove the fired cases and to reload. Holding the fore-end with the left hand and sliding it in front of the tip of the fore-end so that the lever could be pulled across with the right hand was clumsy although the gun was firmly held.

The major problem was the fact that with the gun open the lever was too far to the right for it to be grasped by the extended fingers of the left hand. The gun had to be released by the left hand to stretch across to pull the lever to a position where it could be closed merely by the contraction of the left hand, the thumb around the fore-end, the fingers on the lever.

This takes a bit of thinking about on paper but a little thought should present the problem fairly clearly. What was wanted was some way of partially closing the lever when the barrels were closed. A sort of semi-snap action. I had not come across this type of Lefaucheux action even in the later types with double grips.

The standard English underlever gun with the lever around the trigger guard has this partial closing action if the lever is fairly free and the barrels are closed firmly. The French are ingenious, they did, when all is said and done, invent the breechloader so I thought it not unlikely that somewhere there would be a Lefaucheux gun with a modification to permit partial closing of the lever to make the operation of the gun during loading much easier.

If you wait long enough something does turn up. It turned up on the first day of the Game Fair at Woburn, not only the first day but the first visitors of the first day. Mr. Bailey and Mr. Tolley. Yes, I did ask if he was any relation of the famous Tolley but apparently not!

At first I thought I was being shown another standard Lefaucheux and it wasn't until I had opened and closed the gun that I realised that this was something just that little bit different; it had a partial snap action and the lever, when the barrels were closed, moved across of its own accord to a position where my fingers could close around it and pull it into place in line with the fore-end. Operation was very considerably eased and with such a modification I could see why the Lefaucheux in this modified form could have lasted for the length of time that it did.

The maker's name, found on the right-hand lock plate, was A. Evreux. I have no listing for this maker and at this stage I have to make it clear that my knowledge of French gunmakers of the second half of the nineteenth century is very meagre. I have few French gunmakers' catalogues (those I have are all post-1945) and very few books on French gunmakers, so I cannot tell you anything about Arquebusier Evreux. However, we can say why the gun has this partial "snap" action. There is a little addition to the usual Lefaucheux "T" action – a small metal piece attached to the front barrel lump by a screw. It is this little extra guide that forces the lever round when the barrels are closed. In later underlever guns this modification appears to have been incorporated into the machining of the lumps themselves but at this stage in development this extra component appears to be necessary.

─────7─────
After Lefaucheux

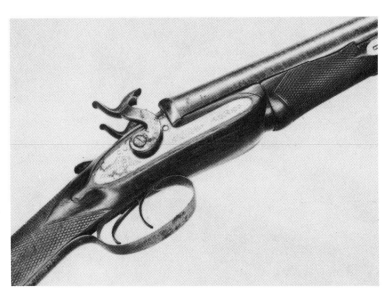

The Westley Richards patent of 1862 covers the "crab joint": a tongue in
the stock enters a recess in the fore-end to protect the hinge.

After Lefaucheux

A PURDEY PINFIRE

Pinfire shotguns have been the most neglected area of firearms study and, for so long, when one appeared, the usual comment was "it's only a pinfire".

Considering the brief period in which they were made in this country a surprising number have survived. One factor could have been that many did not wear out; they became technically obsolete and, even more damning, unfashionable.

The dates we have to use as guides are the famous one of 1851 when the Lefaucheux was exhibited in London, and perhaps 1861, the date usually given for the introduction of the central-fire cartridge by Daw. The dates are given as guides since there is little

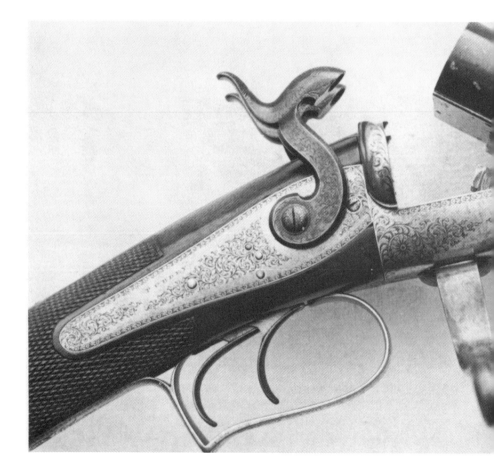

doubt that some pinfire guns were in use before 1851; certainly many were in use after 1861, and, indeed, were manufactured after this date. When the last pinfire was produced is difficult to say, but I would put forward as a claimant a pair of pinfire guns made in 1896 for Charles Gordon by John Dickson and Son, Edinburgh. Few gunmakers had clients as eccentric as Charles Gordon and these guns could well have been among the last pinfire guns made in Britain!

But to return to the pinfire illustrated. This is by James Purdey and according to the number it was made in 1858. A noticeable feature is the "square-backed" trigger guard, a style which was quite popular about this time. I have a John Dickson pinfire of 1863 with a similar guard, and this once again demonstrates the never-ending interest in firearms, since but a short time ago I was writing about guns which had square *fronts* to the trigger guards.

Quite apart from the obvious styling of the Purdey pinfire, a closer look will reveal something else of interest. The guard is arranged so that the underlever curves around it; so here we have one of the earliest "improvements" to the original Lefaucheux

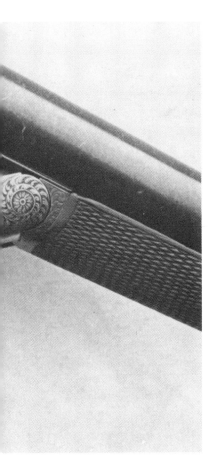

Few pinfire guns can be dated; however, this one by James Purdey can. It was made in 1858 and although it has a rotary underlever the locking is with a single "bite".

system where the lever, if you remember, lay along the fore-end. However, the Purdey is not all that technically advanced since it is but a single "grip" action. There is one barrel lump and this has one slot or "bite" and there is no other bolting employed. Later pinfires were made with the "English" rotary under-bolt with two barrel lumps and two bites – the so-called "double-grip" action.

The Purdey is nevertheless a splendid example of the pinfire as made by one of the best makers in the country. It is graceful, tastefully engraved and typical of the period as regards the style of the hammers and the fences. Later pinfire guns have slightly more graceful hammers – not as heavy in the nose – and the fences in these later guns are treated a little more elaborately.

The important fact about this gun is the date. We know when it was made and so this helps date other guns of a similar style for which the date of manufacture had been lost. Such a gun as this would have been sold in a two-tier case, the gun itself in the top lift-out compartment along with cleaning rods, loading tools etc., whilst beneath the

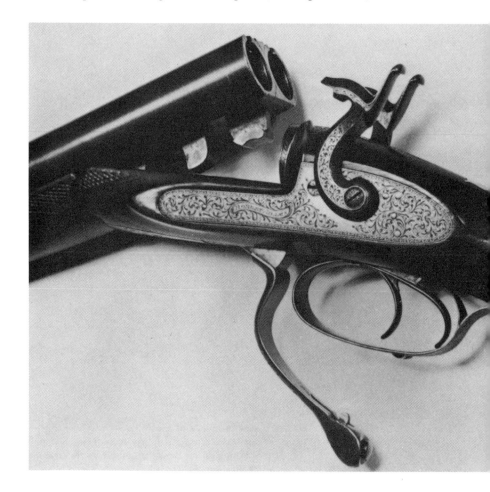

op section would be a compartmented section to hold a supply of pinfire cartridges. Some day perhaps we will be able to have a page full of pinfires to show how they developed over the brief years of their popularity.

THE ADAMS PINFIRE

To those with an interest in firearms the name "Robert Adams" means a percussion revolver, for Robert Adams was the "Colt" of England. In Patrick Edward Dove's delightful little book *The Revolver, its Description, Management and Use: with Hints on Rifle Clubs and the Defence of the Country* is an engraving of Robert Adams loading his pistol. The engraving shows a typical Victorian gentleman, frock coat, high starched collar and a superb "lum" hat. Whatever this gentleman promoted one has the feeling that he could be trusted. Certainly it is difficult to imagine that this staid

Double pinfire shotgun by Robert Adams, made under his patent No. 285 of 1865.

and respectable gentleman leapt to his feet during a lecture given by the famous Colonel Colt at the Institute of Civil Engineers and, producing his revolver from his pocket, brandished it before the assembly in an endeavour to divert attention to his revolver and its merits when all present had attended to listen to Colt puff the merits of *his* revolver. In sharp contrast to the wealth of literature available on the life and activities of Samuel Colt there is little information to be had regarding Robert Adams

He first attracts public attention in 1851 in connection with this exhibit at the Great Exhibition and, of course, his later encounter in November 1851 with Colt. There was also his patent self-cocking muzzle-loading percussion revolver for which he is best known and this patent was a "master" patent in that it covered the basic principle of making the revolver frame and barrel in one piece. The exact relationship between Robert Adams and George and John Deane is difficult to ascertain; Adams was probably the manager of the Deane's workshop until he was taken into partnership in the fateful year of 1851.

The partnership, Deane, Adams, Deane lasted until 1856, Robert Adams subsequently promoting the London Armoury Company. His association with this company lasted for some three years and we then find him advertising from 76 King William Street, London and describing himself as the manufacturing partner of the late firm of Deane, Adams and Deane and "Maker to the Royal Family". Naturally percussion revolvers are advertised but also included is a shotgun.

The advertisement of 1863 refers to "the new breechloader" and from the illustration there is little doubt that we are looking at a representation of the Adams patent breechloader of 1860, a weapon similar in all essentials to that shown here.

This gun is of pleasing form and is fitted with a grip safety. The pinfire hammers are particularly attractive but it is the method of breech closure that is of specific interest. As can be seen the rear lump or "stud", as the patentee calls it, has curved projections on either side. These projections are engaged by the forked end of the pivoted under lever which, when in the upper position locking the barrels, is retained in position against the trigger guard by a button thumb catch.

At the same time Robert Adams patented a special "plug" to allow a pinfire gun to be used as a muzzle loader. To the best of my knowledge none of the plugs has ever come to light; naturally one wonders if this device was ever marketed.

How many of the Robert Adams pinfire breechloading shotguns were made is difficult to assess. Those which have been encountered bear the King William Street address although some must have been sold from his premises at 40 Pall Mall to which he removed in 1865.

Exactly when Robert Adams left not only the premises in 40 Pall Mall but also the gun trade is difficult to discover, for some time after 1866 he vanishes from the London gunmaking world into an obscurity as dark as that from whence he came. A very considerable amount of work has been done by the people whose interest lies in this period but little else concerning Robert Adams and his activities has come to light. His name will be remembered for as long as examples of the Adams percussion revolver exist and it is in connection with his revolver patents that he is best known. Nevertheless, I feel that the shotguns which also bear his name should not be ignored and I have to thank Dr. R. A. F. Gilbert of Brora, Sutherland for his kindness in letting me see the gun and also for the photograph.

THOSE CUNNING CRAFTSMEN

can think of several guns where an idea was just not good enough to survive. Let us have a look at a modern side-by-side double shotgun and the problem of how to load and unload. This was much easier in the days of muzzle-loading; one way only – in at the front end. With breech closure the barrels could be slid forward and the breech backwards (the French liked this idea). The barrels could be swivelled sideways, the breech also. They could be hinged either up or down and although guns have been built with each of these methods, the one that appears to have been most successful is the downwards hinged barrel.

Even if we ignore all the other systems and concentrate on the downwards hinged

The Adams had an inverted "T" lump. On this pinfire by Ronge the "T" is on the lever, not the lump, which as you can see is cut away to accommodate the "T" lever.

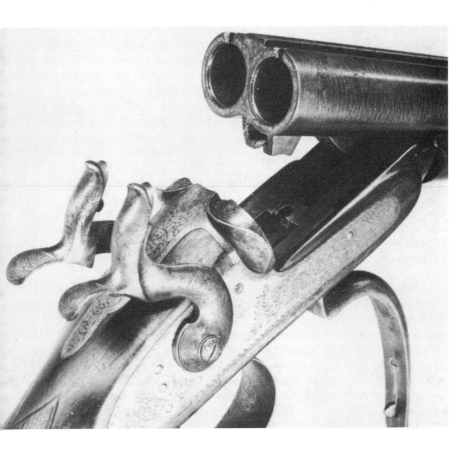

barrel, think of all the many ways there could be of locking the barrels to the action body. Think of them all and you can be almost certain that someone has thought of the idea before you!

This is where Alan Hopwood comes into the picture. He had written to me and suggested that he call and bring his gun with him since it was of special interest. Now the gun is not a best London make, nor is it fully engraved. It was made in Liège Belgium around 1860 at a guess, and it is pinfire, not central-fire.

In the picture the hammers are cocked, of course, since this is a pinfire and they have to be at least on half cock before the gun can be opened. The slots for the pins of the cartridges can be seen in the breech end of the barrels and the "push forward" underlever, which curves neatly round the trigger guard, can also be seen. There is little spring-loaded lock on the lever which engages a slot in the guard and has a "bar in the wood" action. (That phrase always makes my mouth water.)

The most interesting feature of the gun is the method of breech closure. The end of the lever which is in the bar has a curved "T" shaped head. Underneath the barrels will be seen two "L" shaped lugs, the lower bars of the Ls facing each other. As the barrel are brought down on to the action bar the underlever is pulled to the rear and the "T" locking piece enters between the lugs under the barrel. There appears to be a slight "camming" action, the proof being that after all these years the breech closure is still quite tight.

There were other systems like this. Adams invented one, but his worked the other way round and few Adams guns have survived. I've never seen another gun like this one. The maker J. B. Ronge Fils, is famous in Liège, but I have never heard of any British gun with this type of breech closure even made under licence.

Apart from the breech closure the Ronge gun is well worth having a look at since does represent pinfire practice very well indeed; in particular the treatment of the fences, which are pure pinfire!

THE LOCK FAST ACTION

The year is 1861. The benefits of the penny post have been enjoyed for 21 years and Victoria still has 40 years to reign. The might and power of Britain had been demonstrated a decade ago, her wealth and skill displayed for all to see at the Great Exhibition. A sorrier spectacle had been the Crimean War, but that had finished five years ago and today you decided to buy a new shotgun.

Although many still use the muzzle loader you have decided to try one of the new breechloaders. The first and perhaps the most important choice you have to make next is, what type of cartridge to use? This is not a matter of shot size or charge but whether you choose a gun for the pinfire, central-fire or combustible case. On the whole you favour the pinfire; you know that it has several disadvantages although you have discounted the possibility of an accidental discharge due to carrying pinfire cases loose in the pocket but you have experienced a slight escape of gas from the hole or channel through which the pin passes and there have been the odd occasions when the pin has been blown out.

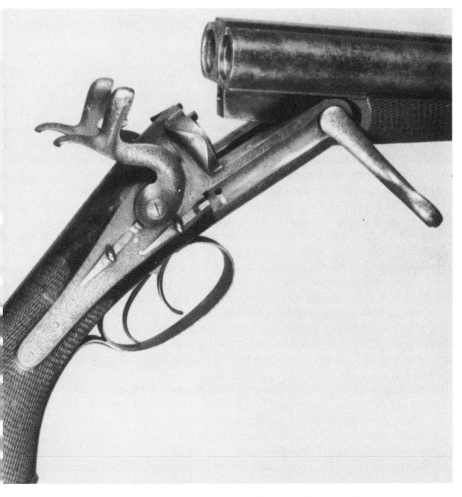

One of the many variants of the Dougall "Lockfast" action. This one is pinfire, with the rearward pointing lever and locking by means of a cylindrical stud which engages the hole in the lump. Bosses on the action face also engage the breeches. Sliding bolts on the lockplates lock the hammers at half-cock and a further bolt locks the lever in the closed position.

On the other hand whilst Mr. Lancaster has offered his central-fire gun they are rather more money than you wish to pay and the new Daw central-fire hasn't been on the market long enough for any serious evaluation to have been made. One point which has caused you concern is the general design of the Lefaucheux gun. Opinions have varied regarding the effectiveness of the locking system and only last year a new design by the celebrated Mr. James Dougall of Glasgow was patented known as the "Lock-fast" and this gun appears to have advantages worthy of consideration, particularly with regard to certainty of closure.

Mr. Dougall is, of course, a provincial maker but he has come to the attention of the sporting public and has this year returned from a visit to Liège where his gun was taken up by the Belgian makers on a royalty basis. The firm is old-established and you have heard rumours that he will be opening premises in London ere long. This then is the gun you intend to buy!

So might the dialogue have gone a hundred years ago between you and your other self. Whether you actually bought a Dougall Lock-fast or not we cannot tell but the story does disclose the dilemma which must have confronted many people half-way through the nineteenth century.

Let's have a look at Dougall's famous lock-fast breech-loading pinfire gun. With hindsight we know that there were two basic types, and the earlier version is shown in the illustration of the actual gun. Back-action locks are employed with a half-cock safety bolt and the barrels are mounted so that they hinge downwards. Not clearly seen are the two discs on the standing breech which fit into recesses formed in the chamber of each barrel. In addition, at the bottom of the standing breech there is a small cylindrical projection which fits into a hole in the barrel lump. There is also a later type of lock-fast action where the lump has a projection which fits into a recess in the standing breech, though the discs are still retained. The method of operation is as follows: the hinge pin carries an eccentric so that when the external lever mounted on the right side of the action bar is rotated, the barrels move slightly forward sufficient to disengage the locking device and permit the barrels to drop down for loading and unloading.

The Dougall was highly thought of at the time and, although the maker's staunch advocacy of the pinfire cartridge did little to stem the tide of progress, his action was later adapted for use with central-fire cartridges.

James Dougall did, in fact, set up in business in London; his shop was at 59 St. James's Street, from 1864 until 1882. His interests broadened to include the letting of shooting properties and he later had interests in the manufacture of smokeless powder.

A safe and satisfactory gun, the Dougall eventually lost out to the later "snap-action" breachloaders and in the opening years of the nineteenth century the firm closed the London premises and retreated back whence they had come, to Glasgow. The business had been established as long ago as 1760 and undoubtedly their greatest period was in the years immediately prior to the First World War when, from their shop at 23 Gordon Street, Glasgow, guns were sold to the gentlemen and nobility proudly bearing the inscription "Maker to HRH Prince of Wales".

THE WESTLEY RICHARDS PINFIRE

Of all the decades in our history, a wise man would choose the 1850s to be young in. (G. M. Young *Victorian England*)

This was the age of invention, of exuberance, of wealth and of the fantastic Crystal Palace, the home of the Great Exhibition of 1851.

After Great Britain the largest single contributor to the exhibition was France and it was the French who exhibited a new breech-loading shotgun which was to revolutionise sporting shooting, the Lefaucheux pinfire gun. Joseph Lang claimed to be the first gunmaker to appreciate the potential of this new gun and subsequently many other gunmakers exercised their skill and ingenuity to improve the method of breech closure. The most widely used system was the rotary bolt operated by an under-lever, a system which, in its semi-snap version, was to survive well into the central-fire period.

The rotary underlever, the original Lefaucheux, the Lepage sliding barrel system and the Dougall "Lock-Fast" all suffered from the same problem, they were relatively slow in operation since all required manual closing. What was needed was a "snap-action" and it was Westley Richards who first produced a snap-action gun in 1858. This gun employed a hook-shaped extension to the top rib which hooked into the breech piece and which was held in position by a laterally moving top-lever. I have never seen an example of this, the first WR drop-down barrel action, and it is difficult to discover how successful this design was.

In a later improvement, which appeared in 1862, the hook extension was abandoned and a "lump" on the barrel entered a recess in the breech piece, the lump having a notch and being locked by a sliding plate which could enter the notch. This system can be easily seen in the illustration on page 165 of the early WR 12-bore pinfire. This is one of the earliest versions since the top-lever is drawn to the rear to withdraw the sliding plate; later versions employed a laterally pivoting thumb-lever and improvements on this design were to be patented in 1864. Today the locking system is known as the "doll's head" extension (see page 165) and is still used in conjunction with Purdey bolts.

The Westley Richards pinfire had other rather interesting features. It was, for example, fitted with bar locks when most of the contemporary pinfire guns used back action lockwork. The "bar in the wood" action was common but WR had original ideas and considered that the joint should be protected. How this was achieved can also be seen from the illustration, the fore-end having a recess into which projected a tongue on the stock. This is one idea which did not enjoy a lasting success but it is most ingenious.

Also unusual, at least to modern eyes, was the fact that the bottom of the breech ends of the barrels were left rounded and the rounded ends bedded on to a central portion of the bar, the wooden "bar" being shaped to receive the barrels.

This action, in one or another of its variations, was very popular and was built by makers other than Westley Richards. The doll's head extension continued to be used as the sole method of breech closure for many years.

THE JONES ACTION

The first gun I was allowed to carry and use, under close and strict supervision, was a double underlever hammer gun. I have a photograph of myself as a quite small boy proudly holding this gun and wearing a cartridge belt in the manner of a bandolier since it was far too large to fit round my waist. What a difference the years have made; now I doubt if I could find a cartridge belt that *would* go round my waist! The photograph does not permit me to identify the gun but I do remember having the action explained to me and from that day on I have always had a soft spot for guns with rotary underlevers. I still use a hammerless gun of this type which has an additional linkage to cock the internal hammers.

Nearly half a century has passed since those days and very often I have had the opportunity to examine hammer underlever guns of friends and chance acquaintances over the years. All too frequently the owner of the gun has been apologetic, not because the gun has hammers but because of the underlever. The guns have been safe, tight and the owners have shot well with them. The only justifiable criticism has been the slowness in reloading compared with a hammerless ejector gun.

The Lefaucheux radically altered the design of the British sporting gun by introducing hinged, drop-down barrels. The barrels, of course, were open at both ends! Today you think little of this, but put yourself in the shoes of a man who for all his life had kept the explosive force of gunpowder in front of a two-inch long solid steel plug, screwed into the breech end of the barrel. All that was to be substituted for this was some paper wadding and a thin sheet of brass. No wonder the breechloader was not an instant success!

Exactly what the pre-1850 Lefaucheux pinfire shotguns were like remains somewhat of a mystery. That the early examples were made in France seems more than likely but what stage the Liège gunmakers started to copy the French designs also remains a mystery. The early examples have a short stubby fore-end, a double bite and a short curved metal lever lying along the fore-end under the barrel. Examples of this type are by no means common and illustrations are rare.

The most commonly encountered version had a straight lever, a metal fore-end hinged to the bar of the action and a smaller lever above the long one which turns in the opposite direction to remove the barrels. Made originally in pinfire, some were converted to central fire and later ones made as central fire guns. Made in France, Belgium, Germany and other European countries, the Lefaucheux action had an incredibly long life, production continuing until the Great War and possibly even afterwards.

When made in this country, as for example by Joseph Lang, the lever was shortened, the fore-end made removable by the standard cross-pin and the stronger original double bite replaced by a single bite. The forward facing lever was not liked in this country and was replaced by a lever which faced the rear and which was curved around the trigger guard. Here we have the beginnings of the rotary under-bolt, and the trigger-guard lever, for on some guns this is what the lever became, the trigger guard not being fitted at all. The main weakness of the action was the single bite

Opposite

The "Doll's Head" extension of the Westley Richards with the earlier
type of pull-back lever. This example dates from 1864.

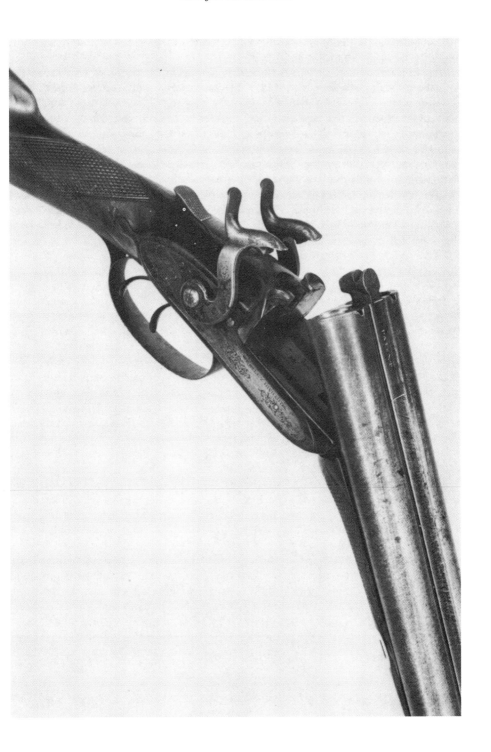

placed quite near to the hinge which resulted in guns built on this plan shooting loose and in some cases fracturing in the bar.

This problem was solved by a Birmingham gunmaker, Henry Jones who is recorded as being in business from 1855 to 1867. His first patent, which covered the double-screw grip, or, as it was known in Europe, the English "T" action, was taken out in September 1859 and then, unfortunately, allowed to lapse in 1862. This permitted the invention to be used by all and sundry and, paradoxically, may account for the wide adoption of what was undoubtedly a highly successful action. Modifications were patented in 1861, and in 1862 Jones patented a totally different type of action along with further modifications to the screw grip action which allowed for the removal of the fore-end when the breech was open. A complex action was patented in 1870 which appears to be the last invention of this quite remarkable Birmingham gunmaker who lived on into the twentieth century. That Henry Jones has not been accorded the fame that was rightly his can be laid at the door of two men. The first, W. W. Greener,

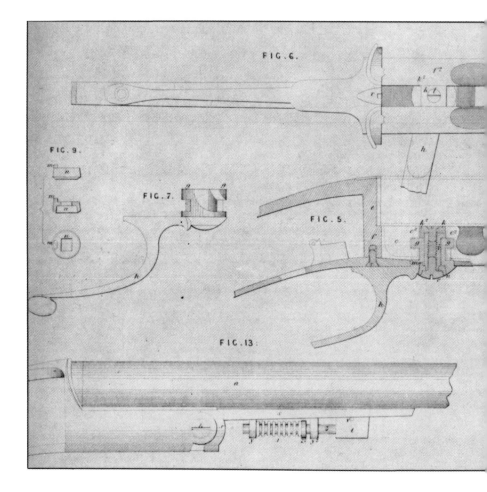

merely states that the gun was "the invention of a Birmingham gunmaker" when he could have easily mentioned the name – "Henry Jones" for there is no doubt whatsoever that he knew about Henry Jones. The second man was J. H. Walsh, the editor of *The Field* who, writing under the name "Stonehenge", again failed to give credit to Henry Jones. In his book *The Modern Sportsman's Gun & Rifle* he states in 1882 that the double grip action is "one of the strongest of all those known to gunmakers". A number of guns built on this action are illustrated but Henry Jones receives no mention.

In their defence one could say that the Jones double-grip was merely a modification of the original Lefaucheux action and Jones himself mentions Lefaucheux in one of his later patents. Against this point of view one can state that the Lefaucheux, in its modified form, had a long life particularly in France. It never achieved the success of the Jones double grip action nor was it ever adapted to the wide range of shotguns and rifles, which, with their rotary underlevers have given such satisfactory service in all parts of the world for so many many years.

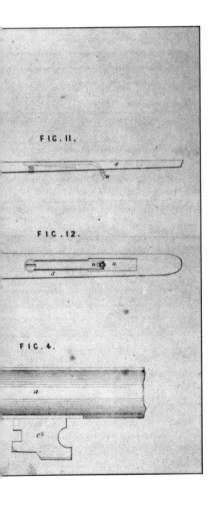

Henry Jones patent No. 2040 of 1859.

The double, offset lumps of this action can be seen with the underlever
and bar-in-the wood styling.

If you use a shotgun with the "double screw grip" then you are using a gun which
employs one of the most famous of all the breech closing actions. Purdey and Anson &
Deeley, Scott and Westley Richards all have their names associated with the shotguns
we use today. Let's give Henry Jones *his* due and give *his* action its rightful name – the
"Jones Action".

A LUMP TO EACH BARREL

My weekly mail brings in all sorts of interesting things; queries, problems, information, pamphlets, old catalogues, photographs and odd assortments of ironware. One
correspondent referred to the advertisement for the Verney Carron side-by-side
shotgun which appeared in *The Shooting Times* Wildfowling number of 30 August,
1979. My attention was drawn to the fact that each barrel had its own lump so that, in
effect, the lumps were side-by-side and not one behind the other as is the case with
most side-by-side shotguns.

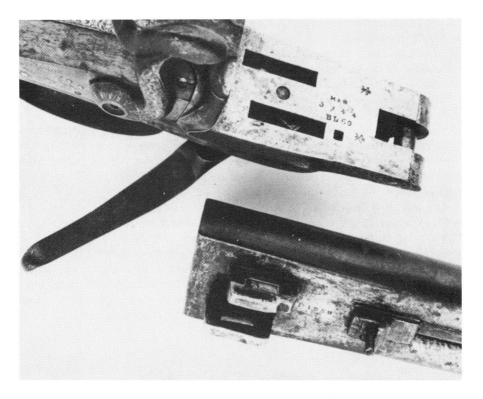

The double lumps under the barrels and the slots in the bar of the action body are clearly seen together with the marks on the flats of the action and barrels.

Most side-by-side shotguns? My correspondent asked if I knew of any other guns which had a similar arrangement of barrel lumps and I was able to tell him that in my experience few things were ever either truly original or exactly the same, and this statement applies to the Verney Carron.

The first shotguns with two side-by-side lumps that I can recall from memory are the German Simpson "Jager" double shotguns. They were hammerless with a top lever and Greener-type top bolting which, unlike the Verney Carron, was their only method of bolting. They were made at the arms factory at Suhl and were on sale before the First World War. Whether Simpson or Jager continued to make this type of gun after 1918 I don't know; my researches do not extend that far.

I could, of course, stop at this stage and say "There you are – at least one other gun with side-by-side lumps", but this is not so. After further research I find a pin-fire gun made by Moore & Harris, even earlier than the Jager. This is the gun illustrated and though I cannot truly describe the lumps as being exactly side-by-side, they are not all that much out of line.

The Moore & Harris gun shown opposite is a bit of a mystery. Although marked

Moore & Harris on the rib and lockplate and in addition being stamped M & H on the bar of the action, no patent in the name of Moore & Harris for this type of construction exists. Moore & Harris was a Birmingham gunmaking firm with premises at 36 Loveday St, from 1840 to 1860. They then moved to the Great Western Gun Works at Constitution Hill in 1861, going out of business in 1864.

There is little to help us here but a closer look at the Moore & Harris gun shows Birmingham proof marks, the number of the gun, 3944, and a rather cryptic BL60.

Under the barrel we find the marks AD 1858 and a search through the patents for 1858 brings to light the provisional patent of Smith, Townsend and Williams. No drawings are annexed so we have to go by what the patent says, "relates to devices for locking the barrel, and consists of providing two lumps on the barrel which are engaged by two wedges operated by a single lever".

Well, does this describe the Moore & Harris gun? I don't know; we have no other marks, no patent numbers and the only description we have of the patentees is that they were manufacturers from Birmingham. What they made we do not know, and, since the patent was a provisional one only, we may now never know. One small clue, however, – where did the German patent originate? There is some evidence that an earlier design was due to a Belgian, and we must wonder whether the Moore & Harris owed its origins to a Continental design, and whether now, with the appearance of the Verney Carron, the wheel has turned full circle, as indeed it often does!

SLIDING BARRELS

We are, I suppose, conditioned in this country to accept the fact that, in order to load our guns, we must hinge open the action – that is, of course, provided we don't use an automatic or repeating shotgun. But I have always been interested in the alternative methods of gaining access to the breech, and one of the systems which has for many years interested me is the sliding barrel.

The most commonly encountered shotgun of this type, in Britain at least, is the so-called Bastin–Lepage. So far, the only justification for the name appears to be because it was used by W. W. Greener in his book, *The Gun and its Development*. In an earlier book, *The Shotgun and Sporting Rifle* by "Stonehenge", published in 1859, a similar gun is described as "Bastin's gun" stating that it has been "very lately made in Belgium". Somebody had been quite quick off the mark, since the Bastin action had been patented only four years previously in Belgium, and certainly guns of the Bastin type of action were made at least until 1861, since Richard Akehurst illustrates a Purdey double 32-bore rifle in his book *Game Guns and Rifles*.

This date of manufacture ties up with the nearest British patent – that of W. J. Harvey of 1860 – and certainly this could have been the design used by Purdey (and others). W. J. Harvey was an Exeter gunmaker and his role in this mystery has been mentioned previously. As yet, no further information which might explain matters has been discovered.

The Harvey patent described two sliding barrel guns – one with the operating lever hinged so that it is drawn to the rear to open the gun, the other with the lever hinged in

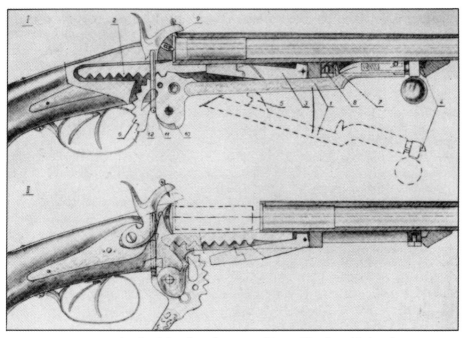

Drawings for the sliding barrel system of Ignaz Wangler of Bohemia.
Guns on this system were actually built – possibly the most bizarre
action ever to go into production.

the opposite direction. Henry Egg made guns on the second system, but I have never
heard of a gun made by the patentee. To be absolutely correct, Egg sold guns carrying
his name but made in Belgium by L. Ghaye of Liège.

Then to make things even more mysterious I was given the chance to inspect yet
another of these sliding-barrel guns by Lloyd of Belper – at the Game Fair, but I have
got no further with this one. Although few of these guns have survived, patents were
taken out for well over 60 different types between 1855 and 1875. If you think about it,
we still use the principle today. One man, J. M. Browning, used it a great deal, his
automatic shotguns and machine guns having sliding barrels!

Just to show how far the sliding-barrel system went, perhaps one of the most bizarre
of the entire group, a truly fantastic double shotgun, was made in the closing years of
the nineteenth century by Ignaz Wangler of Bohemia. The gun is centre-fire but has
additional pins on the hammers to extract the cartridges. Although I have never seen
such a gun, I imagine it must have been a truly extraordinary piece of apparatus.

A SLIDING EGG

Earlier I described the gun-making family of Egg. The Swiss founder of this

Double pinfire shotgun by Henry Egg, with a very neat sliding barrel system.

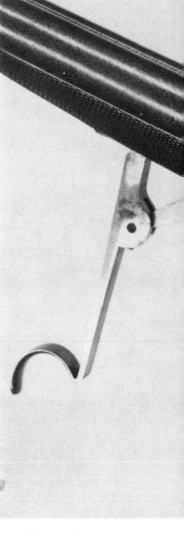

remarkable firm was Durs Egg, but the name on the gun featured here is Henry Egg. Durs Egg started in business in London in 1772 but died at No. 1 Pall Mall Colonade in 1831 aged 83.

Henry was one of the later Eggs and city directories show that he established himself at No. 1 Piccadilly in 1851 and remained in business until 1869 when the firm was taken over by Henry William Egg.

The double shotgun signed by Henry Egg is, as you can see, a pinfire of the highest quality with back action locks. There are two things about it which are unusual. The first is obvious – the barrels slide and do not "drop" down. In the mid-nineteenth century there were a number of shotguns built on this principle. Some bear famous

names, others are less well known, but all I have seen and handled have been of good to very good quality.

The sliding barrel system has prompted numerous questions, but, if you think about it, it is one of the more obvious ways of introducing self-contained cartridges into the breech of a barrel. Look at it from the simple point of view. How do we close up the ends of the barrels on a breechloading gun? The solutions are really few.

If we discard the obvious, screw plugs, we can have a hinged flap such as the Remington Rolling Block. We can have a hinged block, which, if at one side, is the Snider. This type of action was also to be found on double guns in a double block hinged on the right hand side. Instead of being hinged the breech block can slide to the rear and this type of action has lasted until the present day and, as the Leve of 1928, was even modified to work as a four-shot magazine double shotgun.

Instead of sliding, the breech block could be hinged to one side and this applies also to the barrels. Instead of sliding them to one side the barrels could slide forward and this system, known as a "glissiere", was employed on pistols and long guns in the days before self-contained cartridges.

The name of the first maker to employ the sliding barrel action on shotguns firing self-contained cartridges is still slightly obscure. The fundamental principle is quite simple, merely have the barrels sliding along a short rail track. The problem comes in finding some way to lock the barrels securely and to have some means of unlocking them and sliding them forward sufficiently to clear the fired case to permit the gun to be reloaded. With all mechanisms of this type the major problem is that of primary extraction. Some sort of strong cam action is needed to free the expanded case in the chamber. This difficulty arose with the straight-pull Ross bolt action rifle; it lacked the camming action of the Enfield in which the initial turning action freed the fired case. If, as well as freeing the fired case, the operating device could also move the barrels, then this would speed up the loading cycle, something that all gun designers tried to do.

With the early capping carbines this primary extraction had not been important since there was no cartridge case to extract. It is likely that since this system, as made popular by Ghaye, Prince, Bentley and others, was adapted for use with breechloading self-contained cartridges, lack of primary extraction was one of several aspects of the design which, in spite of a number of attempts at improvements, caused the system to be abandoned.

The earliest of these actions appears to be that patented by Bastin Freres but never protected by patent in this country. The earliest British patent was that of Harvey. James Purdey appears to have made a number of guns on the first principle in about 1861, and the Henry Egg, made on the second principle, at first looks as though it was made in this country; but this is deceptive. A close look at the action reveals not the name of Bastin Frères of Liège, but L. Ghaye of Liège.

A close look at the breech end of the barrels shows that there is no extractor and, since this is a pinfire gun, extraction is achieved by indents under the nose of the pinfire hammers which engage the pins of the pinfire cartridges. As the barrels move forward the cases are held back by the pins. The system was not entirely satisfactory and the prudent man would have a pinfire pocket extractor which could be used over the projecting pin and, if this failed due to case separation, then the paper tube could be removed from the chamber with the aid of the tool.

There were centrefire sliding barrel guns, and one with the name Henry Egg on the lockplate and barrel is so similar to the pinfire example that I am tempted to conclude that it is a conversion. This centre-fire has an extractor which withdraws the fired cases about $\frac{3}{4}$ in. from the chambers. This allows the gun to be opened without the cartridges being completely withdrawn and perhaps allows for some degree of primary extraction since the lever is well open before the extractor is engaged.

The central-fire Egg poses a number of problems. It is not marked with any maker's name other than Egg. It could have been made by Egg following the pattern of the earlier L. Ghaye, or, alternatively, the maker's name could have been removed during the conversion work.

There can be little doubt that sliding barrel guns gave the user more confidence in the safety of the system than did the early drop-down barrel guns, but in use the sliding barrel gun had disadvantages which could be neither eliminated nor improved upon so that the system, at least as far as British gunmakers were concerned, proved to be a cul-de-sac, although sliding forward and drop-down barrel actions such as the Dougall enjoyed great popularity before being finally discarded.

SLIDE FORWARD BARRELS

The Game Fair always produces some surprises and the 1978 Fair was no exception. I have, in the past, mentioned and illustrated a type of shotgun action which has always interested me – the "slide forward barrel". We have covered, at one time or another, all the systems which have been tried, but the slide forward barrel system is the one with perhaps more than a little mystery attached to it!

The gun which was brought to my tent this year was one which I have been waiting for, a Purdey pinfire owned by Mr. Donaldson. From the number, this gun was made in 1861 and is, in fact, very similar to the pinfire Purdey double 32-bore rifle which Richard Akehurst illustrates in his book *Game Guns and Rifles*. Akehurst, as most writers, describes the action as "of the Bastin–Lepage" type and shows the barrel in its forward position.

To explain the system, the fore-end is of metal, and, as the lever at the front of the fore-end is unlatched by depressing the inner lever, the operating lever is swung down and to the rear, moving the barrels forward along the fore-end as though they were on rails. The forward motion is enough to permit the removal of the fired cases and the reloading of the chamber.

Previously the history of the sliding barrel has been covered and to those who built and used guns in the mid-nineteenth century the system must have been quite attractive since it would provide one of the most needed qualities that men accustomed to "solid" muzzle loaders would have sought, strength.

Today it is difficult to appreciate what a lifelong user of a muzzle loader must have felt when asked to use a gun which "broke" in the middle. When open, many of the breech-loaders were loose and certainly some of the early bolting systems could not have given rise to a great deal of confidence. With the sliding barrel system, however, there was the comfort of a solid breech and a sturdy method of holding the barrels in position on the stock coupled with the long locking lever.

The system of the Purdey is that patented by W. J. Harvey of Exeter in 1860. As explained previously the Harvey patent covers two types of lever; one hinged so that it

Overleaf
The Purdey "sliding barrel" double pinfire shotgun.

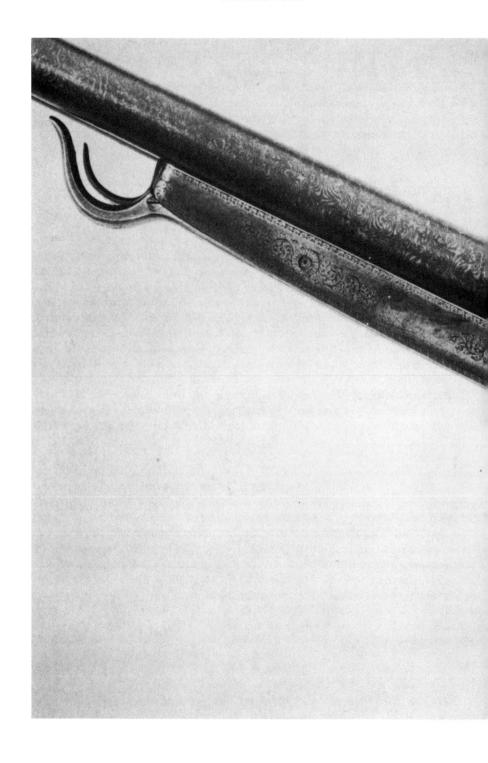

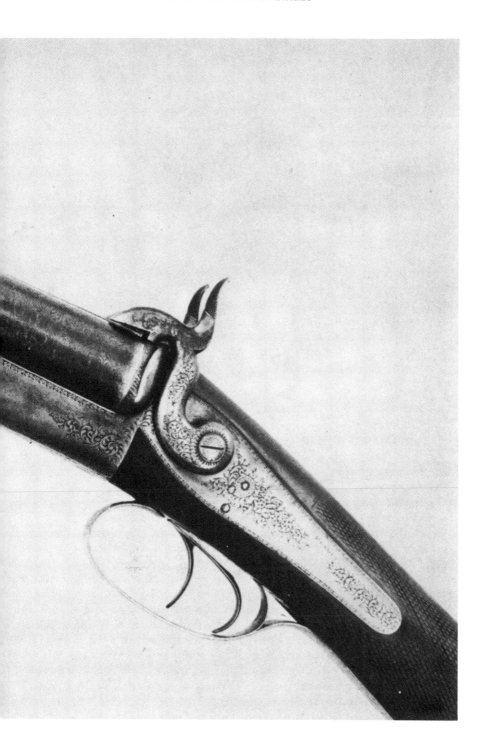

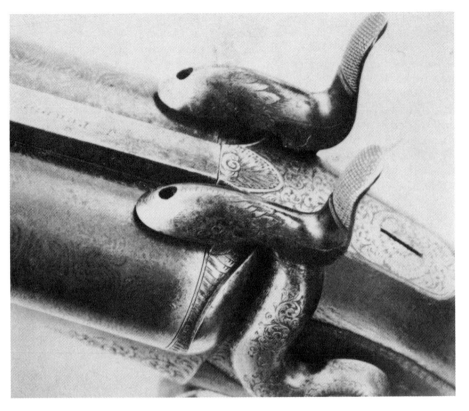

Close-up of the Purdey pinfire hammers showing the holes in the hammer
noses.

has to be pulled downwards and to the rear (as in this example), and the other where
the position is reversed and the lever is opened from the breech end.

In 1862 Joseph Needham patented a number of systems employing sliding barrels,
but I have yet to encounter one which was in production. In the same year Jefferies
patented his system which was a variant employing a laterally-moving barrel, and in
1863 the Purdey bolt, still used today on the majority of side-by-side double guns, was
patented, although employing an underlever and but a single bite.

The sliding barrel system continued to intrigue gunmakers and several more
systems appeared, but how many were actually manufactured is difficult to discover.
Throughout the 1860s the drop-down barrel system dominated but in 1865 James
Purdey patented improvements on a sliding barrel system which also employed
extractors. A number of patents for sliding barrels, at times combined with downward
movements as well, continued to appear but most were of Continental origin and few
appear to have gained favour in this country.

One aspect of the Purdey which is very interesting is the little hole which can be found in the nose of each hammer. How this was used is not absolutely clear. The intention appears to employ the hole to engage the pin of the pinfire cartridge and withdraw the fired case from the chamber. That this can be done is not doubted, since the front position of the hammer nose is nearer to the barrel than is the rear – what is unknown is whether or not the system was "automatic". Did the hole engage the pin when the barrels moved forward, or did one have to move the barrels forward with the pin on half cock and then lower the hammer nose to engage the pin and continue to move the barrels forward? The only way to check would be to put the system to practical trial. This was not possible at the Game Fair but perhaps Mr. Donaldson might try it if he has not done so already! We are still no nearer to the mystery of where Mr. Harvey of Exeter comes into the story and whether or not we would be justified in calling this type of action a "Harvey" action instead of a "Bastin–Lepage" action. Still we have learned something new – the intriguing pinfire extractors. Are there any other guns with similar pinfire hammers?

REES L. LLOYD OF BELPER

I received a letter from Mr. Rod Sykes, who told me about an interesting shotgun he had recently bought. Mr. Sykes lives some distance away from me so it was arranged that we should meet at the Game Fair in Wales. All went well and we did, in fact, meet at that memorable Fair, where I was able to take a photograph of the gun, the one reproduced overleaf. From this photograph it is pretty obvious that here we have a pinfire shotgun in extremely good condition and from my notes, taken at the time, the condition appears to be original and not the result of a hasty rebuild.

Also, to those discerning readers with a critical appreciation of quality, it will be obvious that this is a gun of quality – look at the triggers, their shape and form, and the shape of the trigger guard, the lockplate and the graceful appearance of the cock. The engraving on the lockplate is also tastefully executed, the drop point well shaped and harmonising with the layout of the checkering at the hand. Important though these matters may be, the truly interesting aspect of this shotgun is the breech closure.

We are, I suppose, in this country well conditioned to the fact that to get the cartridges in and out of our double-barrel shotguns we open the guns at the back end and hinge the barrels downwards. A little thought will show that this is not the only way to get the cartridges in and out of the chamber. One maker of shotguns – Darne – who is well regarded in this country and highly regarded in his own, has used another method quite successfully for many years. In France the shooter is used to the fact that his shotgun barrels don't move but the breech end of his gun does. An alternative is to keep the breech end fixed and move the barrels, not downwards as we do but to slide them forward, along a sort of tramline if you like.

One hundred years ago, before the almost total domination of the mechanics of the shotgun by the drop-down barrel (another French invention!), many inventors, but fewer gunmakers, gave considerable thought to forward-sliding barrels and many of the great names in British gunmaking, including Purdey, built guns on this principle. However, I have not been able to discover any other shotgun built on the lines of the

Lloyd of Belper gun. The system is delightfully simple. A projection at the breech end of the barrels enters an orifice in the standing breech and, when fully home, is locked by means of a transverse bolt. Since the gun is a pinfire we do not have to concern ourselves with needless complications like extractors or ejectors and the whole system seems to be entirely satisfactory and delightfully simple.

Who, then, was the inventor of this system? For a start we can try the name on the lockplate – Rees L Lloyd. A prolonged and diligent search brought no information to light on Mr. Lloyd; a very much longer search for a system similar to that used on the Lloyd gun was also unproductive. The patient search having proved to be fruitless I had to write back to Mr. Sykes and tell him the sad news – no information at all on Rees L Lloyd and no information on a patent that might help establish where and when the gun was made. In effect we were exactly where we had started, with merely that name on the lockplate, and the town of Belper.

Later in the year I had another letter from Ron Sykes. In response to my suggestion he had been to Belper and had learned that the only Rees L Lloyd recorded was minister at the Unitarian Chapel from 1845 to 1885. The librarian, Mrs. Robson, could find no reference to his sporting activities although there is no reason to suppose that

Slide forward barrels are used on this pinfire signed by Rees L. Lloyd,
Belper.

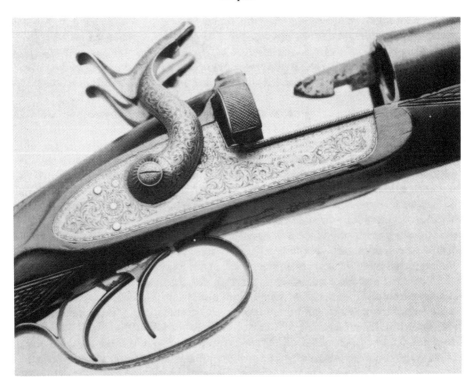

because Mr. Lloyd was a minister he would have no interest in firearms; one has only to think of a very famous sporting parson, the Rev. Alexander Forsyth, for there to be nothing strange in a gunmaking minister in Belper. However, there was no evidence at all to connect Mr. Lloyd with the gun that bears his name and further research by Mr. Sykes brought to light the granddaughter of Rees L Lloyd, and this lady, when questioned, could provide no useful information.

We are therefore confronted by two possibilities – either the sporting activities of Mr. Rees Lloyd were well disguised and unknown to his friends, associates and descendants, or there was another Rees L Lloyd in Belper who still awaits discovery. The shotgun is a very fine one, the action most interesting, and the history both intriguing and mystifying. Perhaps some day the answers will be known.

PINFIRES ARE FUN

Many years ago I started to collect pinfire shotguns. The reason for this was that I simply didn't have enough money to collect good centre-fire guns of the same quality, and muzzle-loading shotguns had already started to rise in price beyond my reach. So pinfire shotguns were collected through financial necessity and, because it was long ago, it was also possible to obtain both loaded and empty pinfire cases. A collection of loading tools followed.

More recently the toll taken of my diminishing stock of pin-fire cases, particularly in the rather odd sizes, for instance 14-bore, has made me a little more careful about firing off the remnants and I could see the day coming when all I would have left would be collectors' items, not really the thing to fire off at random. That was until the 1980 Game Fair at Welbeck.

Normally I don't like to write about things unless I have tried them out myself, so with the proviso that this information is passed on in good faith but without any guarantee, here is a way that the pinfire shotgun can be kept going.

The absence of a self-contained cartridge was, of course, one of the reasons why both muzzle loaders and that rather rarer breed, the breech-loading cap-lock rifle, could be fired since both could be loaded with "home-made" components (except for the caps). With both pinfire and central-fire guns and rifles the problems are greater and considerable ingenuity has been employed in the past, with the expenditure of a great deal of time and effort, to get guns and rifles shooting again when commercial stocks of cartridges have become exhausted. In these columns we have discussed the making of 8- and 4-bore cartridges – now let us make some pinfire ones.

Mr. Fearn showed me an interesting pinfire reloading tool and then a pinfire case, a *plastic* pinfire case with a star crimp. The case has been modified by introducing a brass cap chamber some 7 mm in diameter and 7.7 mm long. The cap chamber (for want of a better term) has a slight rim and it has a 5 mm diameter hole drilled into it to receive a percussion cap. The end of the chamber has a V-shaped cut which allows the flame from the cap into the case proper. A hole is then drilled in the plastic case for the pin. The original pins were made from 2 mm diameter brass wire; Mr. Fearn uses 2 mm

If you don't have any pinfire cases, this modification of the modern all-plastic case could be the answer if you wish to use your pinfire shotgun. The centre-fire primer system has been removed and a small hole drilled in the case. Two items are needed: a pin and a new cap chamber.

diameter iron wire which seems to serve as well. His pins are slightly shorter (by 3 mm) than the original pins which on my measurements average about 22 mm.

The cap chamber can be left in the case but the cap itself cannot be removed without withdrawing the chamber after removing the pin. On the original pinfire case if the pin was withdrawn the fired cap would fall out and a new one could be placed in position by the use of the standard pinfire reloading tool. Mr. Fearn's modification to the original design means that the plastic cases with his cap chamber can be reloaded merely by using a good pair of pliers and an old ball-point pen to push out the cap chamber.

My first attempt to duplicate the "Fearn plastic pinfire" went astray because I had not modified the rim diameter. On average, centre-fire rim diameters are about 1 mm larger than pinfire; this is because the centre-fire rim is used to extract or eject the fired case, a duty not expected of a pinfire. If you look closely at the breech end of a pinfire gun barrel, you will see that the recess for the rim of the case is vestigial. You will have to modify the rim of your plastic case to suit, otherwise you will not be able to close the gun. When you come to load your cases they should first be primed and then the pins should be seated. Here you must be careful not to fire the pin during this operation and this is where the original pinfire loading tool came in useful since it seated the pin to the correct depth.

Then use *black powder* only. No pinfire to my knowledge has been nitro-proofed;

keep the loads light since the gun you are likely to be using is vintage to say the least. Do not exceed 3 drms. of black powder and $1\frac{1}{8}$ oz. of shot. Start with perhaps $2\frac{1}{2}$ drms. of powder and 1 oz of shot. Have your pinfire checked by a competent gunsmith for wear in the barrels or damage, and make certain that the action is sound.

Again, a word of warning. This system will allow a sound pinfire gun of good quality to be used with lightly-loaded black powder cartridges but neither I nor Mr. Fearn nor the publishers can accept any responsibility for damage to the gun or to the person of anyone who attempts to repeat the experiment!

GASQUOINE & DYSON OF MANCHESTER

Interest in Manchester gunmakers dates back to some photographs sent to me by Bill McGuire of East Wenatchee, Washington, U.S.A., of his gun by William Griffiths. Several articles on the Mancunian makers followed and it became obvious that during the nineteenth century Manchester had produced a number of gunmakers who sold guns of quite outstanding quality.

More data on the Manchester makers came from readers of my magazine articles, among whom I have to thank Roy Jacobs for his not inconsiderable help. Then came a letter from Canada, from Dr. Warwick who told me he had a double pinfire shotgun by Gasquoine & Dyson, Market Place, Manchester. I learned that he wished to dispose of the gun and I most certainly wanted to see it. I was aware of the existence of this firm (the name is spelled variously, Gasquoine – Gascuione – Gascoinge) and was very interested to see an example of their work, hoping to find another gun of similar quality to the Griffiths.

The gun was, however, several thousand miles away and, in any case, I could not buy it myself. Then I had a bright idea! A Canadian friend, who is a gun collector, lives partly here and partly in Canada.

He purchased the gun, brought it to this country and a short time later I was able to see and handle it and, with the kind permission of its new owner, photograph it.

As you can see (overleaf), it is a double pinfire with back action locks and underlever "Jones" action. It is of very good quality, in particular the quality of the engraving on the lock plate is quite delightful as is the shape and form of the lever.

Close examination of the hammers reveals a feature of particular interest. The nose of each has what one might call an "apron". I have not seen an apron fashioned in so pronounced a manner before and I wonder if this was a feature of all the pinfire guns made or sold by the firm?

The reason for this feature is obvious to anyone who has used a pinfire. The volume of gas which escapes past the pin – and then leaves the gun through the pin notches in the top of the barrel – is quite considerable. I had one pinfire, that had seen considerable use, in which the escape of gas from reloaded pinfire cases was such as to bring the hammers back to halfcock!

Gasquoine & Dyson are one of the Manchester makers about whom I know very little – except that they made quality pinfire shotguns. Their first address is given in the directories as 1 Blue Boar Court and they were at this address from 1846 to 1852. There

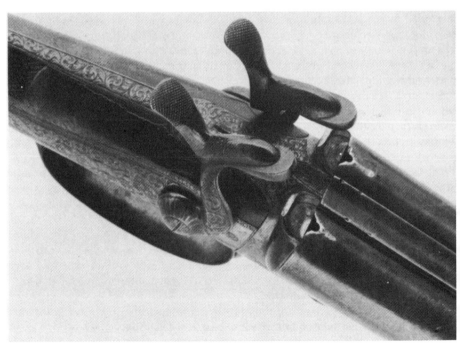

is a gap of two years before they again appear, this time at 26 Market Place which is the address on their pinfire gun No. 1602. They are listed at this address from 1854 to 1864 and then vanish from the written record. However, there was a William Gascoigne working at Albert Street from 1857 to 1869 who is listed as being at Market Place in 1868. In spite of the different spelling there could have been some connection but what it was we may never know.

A search has shown no other gunmaker at 1 Blue Boar Court after 1852 although prior to the arrival of Gasquoine & Dyson at this address William Willoughby Shaw sold guns and crossbows as far back as 1810 from No. 1 Blue Boar Court.

It would be interesting to learn if more guns by Gasquoine & Dyson have survived. I would like to know if they are pinfires and if they have the extended "apron" round the hammer nose.

THE BIRMINGHAM GUN TRADE IN 1868

Some years ago I did a series of articles on the Birmingham gun trade and the kindness and help I received from all the people I met during the time I spent in Birmingham remains a pleasant and lasting memory. Because of the limitations imposed by time I was largely restricted to one or two streets in the remaining part of what had been the Birmingham Gun Quarter. Of these, Price Street was the one most thoroughly investigated with a foray into Bath Street where Bailons Ltd. remained the sole survivor in what even I had known many years ago as a flourishing area. Weaman Street, Whittall Street, Sand Street, St. Mary's Row and Loveday Street had all been part of a Birmingham now long vanished and of a way of life which must be almost extinct.

Many of the places I visited could trace their ancestry back for many years but most began in the second half of the nineteenth century. The height of the demand for arms was in the 1860s due to the American Civil War when Birmingham supplied both sides and, in addition, became involved in the re-equipping of the British Volunteer forces. By 1871, the demand for arms, created by the Franco-Prussian War, had increased the number of gunworkers in Birmingham to nearly 6000.

In 1868 there were thirty-four firms engaged in gun work in Bath Street. Weaman Street had seventy; Whittall Street – 44; St. Mary's Row – 10; Sand Street – 8 and Loveday Street – 36.

Bath Street can be taken as being fairly representative, although I am more familiar with St. Mary's Row. Here No. 11 fronted the street with a central archway giving

Top left
A high quality pinfire double gun by Gasquoine & Dyson of Manchester.
Bottom left
The "aprons" around the hammer nose are distinctive. Some guns with this feature have the apron pierced with a small hole.

access to a back courtyard. The story I was told many years ago was that this house had belonged to a doctor in the opening years of the eighteenth century, but that as the gun trade had moved into the St. Mary's district around the old church of St. Mary's the doctor had taken his practice elsewhere and the house and the outbuildings had been converted into workshops.

Originally the house had been used part as dwelling house and part as storeroom for the master gunmakers. The workers rented out "shopping" behind the "frontage" and whole congeries of gun workers became established, and as they outgrew the original buildings others were put up on a similar plan; the workshops in one, two and three storeys, often with outside stairs, grew up around back courts so that it was possible to have an entire gun finished within a group of independent craftsmen.

One of the few "pictures" of the gun quarter in the 1860s is to be found in Allen's *Industrial Development of Birmingham and the Black Country*. This description is one which brings to mind my own visits to St Mary's Row just after the last war and I quote it in full:

> A passage from the main street communicated with a court-yard, from which two blocks of two-storeyed buildings rise, facing one another; and at intervals staircases lead up from the courtyard to the workshops, of which the buildings are entirely composed. Each shop consists of one or two small rooms, in which the various operations in connection with the setting up of guns are performed. In one shop, two men will be found engaged in barrel-browning; in another a single workman is employed in shaping gun stocks from a pile of roughly cut blanks, delivered to him by the master gunmaker. Elsewhere a lock filer is working with one assistant and in another shop, leading from the same staircase, an engraver and his sons carry on their trade.

The writer goes on to describe how the "names of the proprietor are chalked on the door" and I can remember thirty years ago seeing scenes exactly as described.

One thing the writer of the 1860s did not do was to give some idea of the sort of people who lived and worked in these conditions. Those I knew were proud, confident men, secure in their highly specialised skills, articulate and knowledgeable about the trade and affairs. But what of the men of 1860–70? Little or nothing has come down to us about them; the only ones who have left a written record are the few who became important gunmakers, second sons of a flourishing business and not representative of the vast mass of the gun trade.

However, recently just one tiny corner of the veil which hides the history of these men has been lifted and we get the merest glimpse of a member of the gun trade in 1868. This is due entirely to Mr. Dutton who kindly sent me a notebook which belonged to his grandfather, and from the extracts given you can tell something of the man who worked in one of the workshops described above as 92 Bath Street in 1868. No. 92 is still there, but the back courts and "shopping" appear to have been destroyed. At these premises there must have been a back court for on 8 April, 1867 Mr. C. Dutton rented workshop premises for one shilling and threepence a week. His notebook starts in July 1868 and from this we find that he is engaged on "screwing and finishing" guns which was a part of the trade involved in fitting trigger guards, trigger

A page from Mr. C. Dutton's work book for the year 1868.

plates and metal furniture to the gun and also finishing the woodwork and doing the chequering where needed.

During the month of August Mr. Dutton did work on nine "Navals" and a number of double "backwork" guns, several "bar" guns and one "single" gun. His income for August came to £2/7/8d. from which we know he paid 1/3d. rent each week.

The book does not list any "outgoings" other than rent, such as gas or candles, coal, and materials and tools of his trade. But it does mention other work for a special customer, Mr. J. Roberts, and we find that Mr. Dutton received 2/11d. each for finishing twenty-six double bar guns which totalled £3/15/10d.

Most of the writing is in truly excellent copperplate and among the pounds, shillings and pence of the accounts one finds "The Wreck of the Hesperus". Then one encounters "Hamlet's Soliloquy on Death" and yet another poem, "Virginians". There is no indication as to whether the poetry was written before the accounts or along with them or after them, or indeed why they were put into the book at all. The book has but forty pages and, although there is much I wish Mr. Dutton had recorded, I must be grateful for what he did write and for showing me that his thoughts were not entirely occupied by the gun trade.

THE CENTRAL-FIRE HAMMER BREECHLOADER

History is bedevilled by dates. We want to know who was responsible, we want to know what he did and how it differed from previous practice and, more often than not, of even greater importance, when did it happen? Some events did happen at a specific and precisely recorded time, other events were slow and gradual, the *calculus of history*, slow in some areas, rapid in others. For example, a hundred years from now someone could well be quite astonished that, in spite of the fact that John Browning patented a locked breech semi-automatic shotgun in 1900, it wasn't until 1903 that production commenced at the F. N. Factory in Liège, and 1905 before Remington produced the Browning as the Remington Model 11. The real surprise would be that such a shotgun is still not used on formal shoots in this country eighty years after it went into production. On the last five days out not only have my fellow guns not used automatic shotguns but there was not even an "over and under" gun to be seen!

A hundred years in the future an earnest enquirer could well ask "What influence on the British shotgun scene did the appearance of Japanese manufactured shotguns have?" If this question was asked today the answer would be quite different depending on whether the question was asked of a member of a syndicate shoot in the home counties or a clay pigeon club in the north of England. What sort of answer would we be likely to get a hundred years in the future?

In this book we are looking at events even more remote in the past and to a great extent we lack the amount of data that the future researcher is very likely to have.

It is for this reason that we can provide the exact date of a patent but not always when that patent went into useful service and the extent to which the idea gained popular acceptance. We do know, for example, that during what we might call the "pinfire period" many held very strong objections to the pinfire breechloader amongst

Safari Press, America's premier big game publisher, regularly releases books on worldwide big-game hunting, wing-shooting, and firearms. Please complete and return this postcard and you will be updated on our new publications. *(Please do not send this post card if you have previously received a book directly from Safari Press, you are already on our mailing list.)*

PLEASE PRINT:

NAME _____

ADDRESS _____

_____

CITY / STATE _____ ZIP _____

COUNTRY _____ TEL (___) ___ - ___

SAFARI PRESS, INC.
P.O. Box 3095
Long Beach, CA 90803-0095, USA

whom we can count the renowned Birmingham gunmaker W. W. Greener. In his book *Gunnery in 1858* Greener stated that "there was no possibility of a breechloader ever shooting equal to a well constructed muzzle loader" and that it was both unsafe and "a very costly affair".

One way to resolve the conflicting opinions so strongly voiced in the sporting press of the period was to carry out trials between muzzle loaders and breechloaders under controlled conditions.

In 1879 the Pettitt pad had been replaced by a device known as the Field force gauge, to test penetration. The trial of 1875 was designed to test the "choke-bore" and that of 1878 was a trial of powder rather than of the gun. That of 1879 was designed to test the relative merits of 12, 16 and 20 bores. There is no mention in any of these later trials of pinfires or muzzle loaders so we must assume that in spite of the fact that both types of gun were still very much in use no maker considered it worthwhile to enter either muzzle loaders or pinfires in the trials.

Exactly what influence these trials had on the gun buying public at large is now difficult to assess, certainly those who came out well were not adverse to recording these successes on the top rib of the guns that they sold. Other makers came to rely more and more on practical results in competitive shooting at live birds and the advertisements of the period record their successes.

Although the 1870s saw the introduction of the hammerless breechloader, hammer guns continued to be used until the turn of the century even by those who could well afford to scrap them or pass them on to the keeper. The hammer guns of the '80s and '90s are amongst the most graceful guns ever built and today the hammer gun is enjoying a new popularity with many of the guns of a century ago seeing use in the field and giving pleasure to their owners.

8
Miscellany

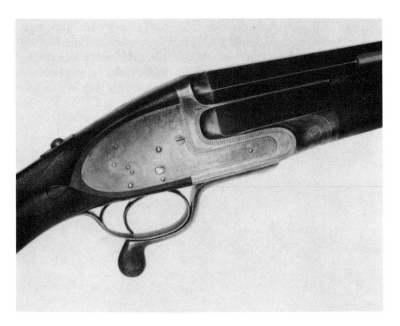

A magnificent single 4 bore sidelock shotgun by James Purdey. Built in 1904 for brass cases, this is an outstanding example of a "big bore" gun.
(Courtesy Hampton Galleries)

Miscellany

SCHNEIDER, PARIS

It would be most interesting to obtain details of the true extent to which the Lefaucheux breech loading pinfire gun had been adopted by the sporting public in Britain in the decade following the Great Exhibition of 1851. I should also like to know how many French Lefaucheux shotguns were in use in Britain prior to their public introduction in 1851. The spread of the breech loader must have been quite extensive in view of the number of pinfire guns which have survived, although I suppose it must be expected that the survival rate will have been influenced by the "obsolescence factor". Many will have survived because they were taken out of use, replaced by centre-fire guns and therefore didn't wear out and get scrapped.

The muzzle loader had been threatened by the French pinfire and it was another French invention, the Schneider breechloader, which threatened the supremacy of the pinfire.

Schneider's original French patent was dated 1858 and then in 1861 François Eugène Schneider obtained a British patent which described a centre-fire gun with snap underlever action and cartridge extractors. This patent was purchased by the well known London gunmaker, G. H. Daw and with the Schneider central-fire case became the "standard" shotgun and the progenitor of the double barrel shotgun of today.

Illustrated is a genuine Schneider central-fire shotgun. This gun is a 16-bore, the

Centre-fire underlever double shotgun signed "Schneider à Paris".

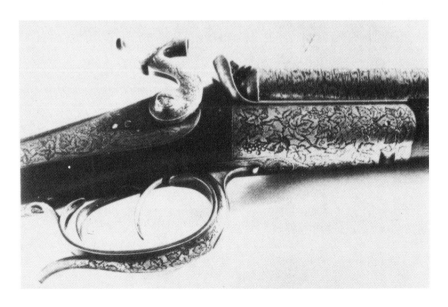

barrels and lock plates being marked "Schneider, Paris," the barrels being marked underneath with the name "Leopold Bernard, Canonier, Paris." Bernard was a barrel maker who gave his name to a special grade of Damascus barrel which was highly regarded by those in "the know".

Just how many Schneider shotguns were either brought into Britain by sportsmen from France or how many were imported is completely unknown. How this example got here we do not know; it may have come to Britain many years after it was made or it could have arrived before G. H. Daw started manufacture of his version of what is an important milestone in the development of the sporting shotgun.

Opinion regarding the Daw was very favourable but I have yet to find anyone giving his opinion on the Schneider, least of all that most vocal of gunmakers, George H. Daw of 57 Threadneedle Street, London.

CENTRAL-FIRE CONVERSIONS

By the early 1860s the Lefaucheux pinfire shotgun loaded from the breech had generally been accepted by shooting men as a decided improvement on the muzzle loader, which, in spite of its lighter weight and proven shooting ability, was fast losing out to the convenience and greater safety of the breechloader. However, all was not well with the pinfire. Although it was accepted that there was no serious danger of an accidental explosion of a pinfire cartridge if carried in the pocket, it would nevertheless be prudent to avoid getting into a situation where such an accidental discharge might occur. After all, did not the pinfire have a protruding pin, which, if struck, would cause the cartridge to go off?

Less dangerous perhaps, but very annoying, was the possibility of misfires. These were not unlikely with the pinfire if the little pin became bent, and misfires were often traced to defects in the pin. There was also the problem of having to place the cartridge correctly in the breech with the pin lying in the correct slot in the chamber. Added to this was the problem of extraction, so that there was a strong case for some improvement.

The improvement came with Mr. Charles Lancaster's breechloader, which was built on the central-fire plan, but due to the special cartridges (which could be obtained only from Mr. Lancaster) and the high price of the gun, the Lancaster was restricted to the wealthy few.

It was left to Mr. George H. Daw of Threadneedle Street to come up with a reasonable alternative – one which was to sweep away the pinfire with all its attendant problems.

The Daw central-fire cartridge was, in all essential respects, much the same as that which we use today and, by 1861, George Daw had a shotgun and cartridge on the market which, although patented in the name of F. E. Schneider, was to be the gun of the future.

But what of those people who had bought pinfires, and bought them not long ago? Were their guns to be put away on one side and forgotten? Fortunately for us, many were. It is to this swift change in cartridge technology that we owe so many scarcely

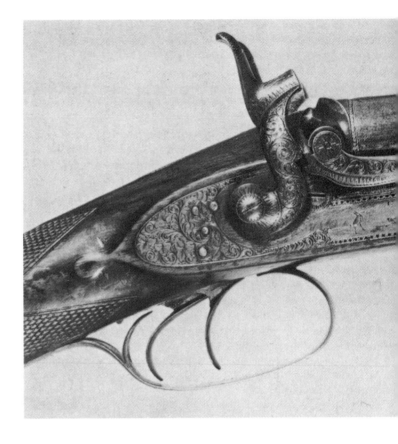

A quality pinfire shotgun converted to central-fire.

used pinfire shotguns which tell us so well, over a century later, what a range of styles had been made, so many in such a short time.

Those less well endowed would have to make do with their obsolete pinfire guns despite the blandishments of the gunmaker eager for new custom. But would they? If the gunmaker of Victorian times could not sell a new central-fire gun perhaps he could earn an honest crust by converting the pinfire into a central-fire gun. By this means he got some work and the owner many more years of useful life from his shotgun.

The gun illustrated is a good example of such a conversion. The original was a pinfire made by Charles Ingram of Glasgow employing Needham's breech fastening. To open the gun the lever on the right hand side of the action is depressed; this unbolts the barrels and at the same time raises the hammer to half-cock. With the pinfire this was important since the gun could not be opened otherwise and even with the central-fire gun it was necessary to raise the hammers to allow the strikers to be withdrawn from the indentation in the central-fire caps. You can see how the hammer nose has

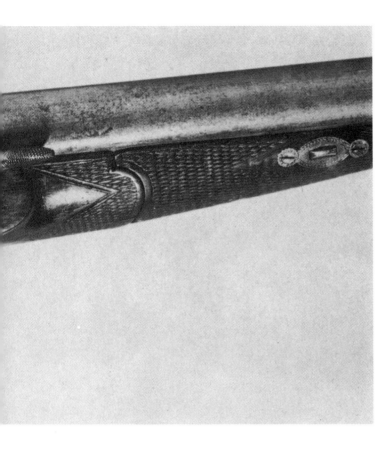

been removed and angled strikers inserted through the fences of the standing breech.

This was a quality gun which doubtless gave its owner many more years of service as a central-fire before it was given honourable retirement. Quite a number of pinfire guns were so converted and, in themselves, they provide a very interesting study of the gunmaker's ingenuity.

THE WESTLEY RICHARDS PATENTS

Every now and again I get a series of photographs which present me with several problems. The first is, which to use? The second is, when? The first question arose when I was given a truly superb set of prints of one of Mr. R. S. Crowe's guns, a Westley Richards hammer gun. Of the three prints which I received I have chosen one which clearly shows more than one of the interesting features of this gun.

A beautifully restored central-fire gun by Westley Richards. Serial No. 12399.

First of all, its number 12399, which dates it at about 1870. The most important feature is the use of the Westley Richards doll's head barrel locking system. For those who are unfamiliar with this system the illustration shows quite clearly the barrel extension or "lump" as Richards called it in his 1862 patent. Also clearly seen is the notch in the lump into which enters a sliding plate, locking the barrel in the closed position. The plate is withdrawn by the top lever which is much broader than the top levers of today but which remained a distinctive feature of Westley Richards guns well into the hammerless period.

Not so easily seen from this angle is the fact that this is a bar-in-the-wood gun. A special feature of the Westley Richards bar-in-the-wood guns of this period is the use of an extended "tongue of wood" which projects into a recess in the fore-end so protecting the joint.

As this is a true bar-in-the-wood gun there are no "flats" on the barrel since there are no flats, in the later accepted sense of the term, on the bar of the action.

The next important feature of this gun is the fact that it is a centre-fire gun. If you look closely there is much that reminds one of the pinfire, in particular the shape of the hammers and the fact that they are, in form and style, pinfire hammers. This can be seen from the length of the hammer nose although, again, from this angle it is not too apparent. An even closer look brings to mind an even earlier muzzle-loading gun and it can be truly said that this particular example shows features of what we might call several "periods".

Pinfire hammers, though they may be, they do strike centre-fire strikers. The system employed is that patented by Westley Richards in 1866. The strikers are in two parts, namely the striker proper, which is in line with the bore, and what Richards calls "the driver", the head of which can be seen in the illustration. Although I have called the extended part of the hammer the nose, Richards calls it the neck. The drivers are thus struck by the neck of the hammer and the nose, or face, can be used for pinfire cartridges. There is no provision at the breech of the barrels for pinfire cartridges and I wonder if guns were made suitable for both types of cartridge? Certainly, the Westley Richards system permits the ignition of both pinfire and centre-fire.

I had hoped to see this gun at the Game Fair but Mr. Crowe and I missed each other. I hope perhaps next time I shall be able to examine it but for the present the photographs are the next best thing.

A DOUBLE, DOUBLE PINFIRE

One of the many delightful features of the 1974 Game Fair was the number of readers who brought guns for me to look at. The range was wide and there were many of considerable interest brought to the stand. I was particularly pleased to have the chance to see the very fine Westley Richards owned by Mr. R. S. Crowe which has just been discussed, and another owned by Mr. R. Birch.

Although Mr. Crowe had supplied a variety of photographs which showed the gun from every angle, when I was looking at this gun with Mr. Roger Lees of the Birmingham Proof House – I noticed something that had not been apparent in the photographs. I was puzzled until Mr. Lees provided me with the explanation.

Mr R. Birch had gone to considerable trouble to bring several guns to the stand, one of which was another Westley Richards gun – No. 10277. Mr. Birch had seen Mr. Crowe's really fine Westley Richards and was a little dubious about showing his example which was older and not in the same fine condition. But his reluctance was overcome, and it was most interesting to compare the two Westley Richards guns. Mr. Birch's gun, which is illustrated opposite, is another bar-in-the-wood action but it had once been a true pinfire. Mr. Crowe's later WR, although exhibiting many pinfire features, had been built as a centre-fire gun.

The Birch WR gun had been converted from pinfire to central-fire by the substitution of central-fire hammers which are much later than the rest of the gun and are also of different styling. The standing breech was altered to take central-fire strikers and because the strikers are not fitted to the gun this work can be seen clearly in the illustration. There is, of course, no extractor, and the way the barrels have been put together is interesting.

The most intriguing feature of all is the fact that the original pinfire slots are still retained in the barrel. On many conversions these slots were filled in. Not only are the original slots still to be seen but there are two additional slots, diametrically opposite. Mr. Birch wanted to know what these additional slots were for and I was able to tell him. Have a look at the photograph and see if you can guess the reason.

Remember that the original locks are used so that they have a reasonably long throw to the half cock in order that the original pinfire hammers clear the end of the barrels when the gun is opened. The gun hasn't got rebounding locks. That is the important point. So, to save time and avoid the need to bring the locks to half cock to permit the strikers to retract, slots were cut in the bottom of the barrels. This dodge means that with the hammers down and the strikers protruding through the face of the standing breech, the barrels can still be opened. Without the slots the barrels would be caught by the tips of the strikers.

If I hadn't had the chance of handling this gun it is likely that photographs which might have been provided would not have shown the extra slots. Also, I have to admit that if Mr. Birch hadn't drawn my attention to these slots I could have missed them, even with the gun in my hands.

One thing leads to another, so back to Mr. Crowe's gun went I, to have another look at the strikers on that gun. No slots in the barrel and no little cuts in the extractor either but something else of interest.

More on Westley Richards

Now to return to the Westley Richards gun owned by Mr. Birch, gun number 10277. Originally built as a pinfire it was later converted to central-fire by the substitution of new c.f. hammers. It was also necessary to provide centre-fire strikers and you will remember that to give clearance to the strikers with the hammers down the bottom of the barrels had a slot cut into the face. This gave the barrels a rather odd appearance – as though the gun had been made for cartridges with two pins opposite each other.

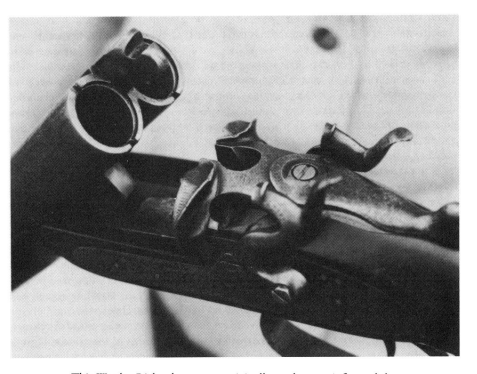

This Westley Richards gun was originally made as a pinfire and then converted to central-fire. The strikers are absent and new c.f. hammers have been fitted, probably at the time of the conversion. The interesting features are the two opposed slots in the barrels.

Most pinfire conversions have the pinfire slots filled in, and if the conversion is well done it is not always easy to tell that the weapon was not made as a central-fire gun.

I mentioned previously that I had been looking at another Westley Richards gun with the owner and with Mr. Roger Lees, proof master of the Birmingham Gun Barrel Proof House. The gun was that owned by Mr. Crowe and which appeared and was illustrated earlier. This photograph, provided by Mr. Crowe, is a very fine piece of work since the gun's serial number – 12399 – can be read as it appears on the extractor.

I had looked at this photograph a number of times and when I was at the Game Fair I had the chance of seeing the gun itself. When Roger Lees appeared he asked me to see the gun and drew my attention to three figures stamped at the top of each barrel. I had overlooked these numbers, and even when my attention was drawn to them I was unable to account for their presence.

I was not kept long in suspense since it appears that Westley Richards were in the habit of marking the barrels with the chamber mouth diameter, in this case 0.815 in. Today this diameter is known as the "underhead diameter" and for a nominal $2\frac{1}{2}$ in. 12-bore the dimension should be between 0.822 and 0.810 in.

The gun was made around 1870, which was before cartridge and chamber dimensions had been standardised, and the fact that Westley Richards had dimensioned the chambers of their gun would help ensure that correct size cartridges were used. It wasn't until 1882 that makers made an endeavour to standardise their cartridges. This seems to have been done by Kynoch and the "under rim diameter" of his 12-bore cartridges was 0.810 in. maximum. Kynoch suggested that the chamber should be between two and four thousandths of an inch larger than the maximum dimension of the cartridge. This size range, or tolerance, ensured that the cartridge would enter the chamber on the one hand but on the other would not split through too much expansion.

I was most interested in this and suggest that owners of early Westley Richards guns check to see if the chamber dimensions on their guns have survived the last hundred years' wear and tear! When I returned home I developed and printed some of my photographs taken at the Game Fair, and was able to study in detail the interesting strikers fitted to Mr. Crowe's gun.

This is an early central-fire and not a conversion. Pinfire-style hammers are fitted, the nose of the hammer being long enough to prevent the barrels from being opened when in the fired position. The strikers are not spring-loaded but, as mentioned before, are in two parts. The striker can be seen protruding through the standing breech and the "driver", as it was called by Westley Richards, is standing proud above the standing breech. Since the hammers have to be drawn to half cock to allow the barrels to pass the nose, the bottom of the barrel has to clear the tip of the striker. This is where the centre-fire conversion employed the little cut-outs. On this gun, however, the strikers have inclined surfaces so that as the barrels pass them, either opening or closing, the strikers are "swept" to the rear. A lot of thought went into the design of this gun and I have to admit that it took a lot of thought to unravel some of the fascinating mysteries. I think that this gun illustrates how important it is to carefully examine early breechloaders since there is often more to them than meets the eye.

ODDS AND ENDS

One of the questions I have been asked about the slots on the barrels of Mr. Birch's Westley Richards gun is: "How do we extract the cartridges without an extractor?" Even if we assume that the little slots already described are needed for the clearance of the strikers we are still left with the problem of removal of a fired central-fire case.

I have a vague recollection of owning an odd tool which, on reflection, could well have been for the removal of central-fire cases where it was not possible to fit extractors to the gun. Such a case would be on the Westley Richards owned by Mr. Birch. I also remember having seen an illustration of an early central-fire shotgun with a tool looking rather like a pair of forceps which could have been employed to remove the fired case. That is why we need the little slots at the top and bottom of the chamber mouth, so that the extractor tool can be used!

CHARLES LANCASTER'S BREECHLOADER

When an important event occurs there is the comforting feeling that someone will be available to record the facts for the future. Experience with the research necessary to provide the historical background to firearms shows that this is not the case, or, if indeed anyone did take the trouble to write down their feelings or impressions, this information has been lost to us. One of the most interesting early breechloading shotguns is that which bears the name of Charles Lancaster of 151 New Bond Street, London. The illustration shows the salient features: back-action hammer sidelocks, rotary underlever. Extractor, yes that's easily seen, but what may not be immediately apparent is the fact that the barrels don't just hinge open, they move forward as well.

You can see the gap between the fore-end iron and the bar of the action. This forward movement allows the massive locking bolt to move forward and clear the recess in the standing breech. Some years ago I illustrated an earlier Lancaster – a 14-

The later Lancaster made for the conventional central-fire cartridge. The massive locking lug at the rear of the barrels can be seen. This locks up under the standing breech when the barrels are closed, and then slides to the rear by the camming action of the underlever.

bore, No. 3628 – in *The History of the Shotgun* which appeared in *Shooting Times & Country Magazine* (July 1967). The Lancaster illustrated here is No. 4900; it is a 3 in. 12-bore with 32 in. barrels and weighs over 10 lb. The earlier 14-bore appears to have been made about 1863, the heavier 12-bore about 1878. The difference in styling is confined to the hammers· which, on the later gun, are more streamlined and when at full cock are not visible in the line of sight; they are also easier to cock. The locks of the later gun are rebounding, but I can't remember whether the locks on the 14-bore were or not.

The original Lancaster breechloader appears to date from 1852 – one year after the Great Exhibition of 1851 where, so we are told, the British sporting world was astounded by the appearance of the pinfire breechloading French Lefaucheux shotgun. If we are to believe what has been handed down to us one year later Lancaster had introduced a "base-fire" cartridge and a shotgun that was, in my present day opinion, vastly superior to the Lefaucheux.

I have to be quite careful here about what I say, and perhaps I should slightly modify my statement since I have neither handled nor fired a Lefaucheux shotgun of the type exhibited in 1851, nor an *original* Lancaster.

It is to be regretted that there is no patent in the name of Charles Lancaster in spite of the fact that the guns bear the legend "Charles Lancaster's Patent" on the bar of the action. Recent research has shown that the Lancaster is based on French patents of 1853 taken out in the name of Auguste Edouard Loradoux Bellford. This gentleman was a patent agent at 16 Castle Street, Holborn, London and part of the patent describes the Lancaster and the illustrations show the sliding barrel (described in the patent as a "moveable sliding breech") which is such an important feature of the Lancaster. The extractor employed by the Lancaster is described as a "moveable chamber mouth" which, one has to admit, is descriptive. A later patent in the name of another patent agent, Richard Archibald Brooman, names as his principal, L. J. Gastinne. This patent of 1862 refers to the cartridges in a drop-down barrel gun being extracted by a "plate" and mentions the Bellford patent of 1853 and that the 1853 patent was "assigned to Charles William Lancaster of New Bond Street, London". A date is given of 22 November, 1856.

From this it can be inferred that yet again the British gun trade owes a debt to the French, this time for one of the strongest and simplest of all the early breechloading actions. Louis Julien Gastinne was a member of the famous French gunmaking house of Gastinne-Renette founded in 1812 by Rene Gastinne.

The conclusion one must reach is that the date given for the introduction of the Lancaster is early, by one to three years. Contemporary comments date from 1859 when the Lancaster "base-fire" cartridge appears to be still in use. No examples of this cartridge are known to me and details of the construction are only known from drawings, one of which is to be found in J. H. Walsh's book published in 1859.

How long the Lancaster cartridge was made and by whom is uncertain since much of contemporary information is conflicting and contradictory. One question which remains unanswered is whether or not the Lancaster required modification to fire the later central-fire cartridges introduced by George Daw in 1861. Certainly the Lancaster continued to be made for use with the true central-fire cartridge for as we have seen the 12-bore No. 4900 dates from 1878.

Contemporary with the Lancaster was the Lefaucheux pinfire, made in Britain by Lang, together with the Bastin pinfire where the barrels slide forward, and the Needham needlefire. Opinion in 1859 was in favour of the Lefaucheux pinfire. Lancaster's gun was regarded as "being exceedingly clever" but was not liked because of the higher price and the fact that cartridges could only be obtained from the maker – Lancaster – whereas pinfire cartridges "could be obtained in all our principal towns".

It may be that there are some more Lancaster shotguns in existence – guns of the type illustrated, that is. There may also be some cartridges and some literature on the gun and cartridge or some contemporary comment. I will be interested to receive any information which will allow a slightly better picture of the events and the situation in the 1850s to be gained.

SLIDE AND DROP DOWN

The Tayside Field Sports Fair of August, 1980 was, for me, a most pleasant occasion. As usual a number of people had gone to the trouble of bringing guns for me to see and several other interesting pieces were made available to me by those with stands. One such gun was a MacNaughton lent to me by The Angus Gun Room of Broughty Ferry, Dundee.

To the student of nineteenth century sporting arms the name MacNaughton must inevitably bring to mind the famous MacNaughton "Trigger Plate" hammerless gun, a design which has been dealt with at length in the past and which will most certainly be dealt with again in the future. The MacNaughton which I had the opportunity of handling and photographing was a rather rarer bird and one which is to be found in a delightfully varied number of guises.

At first sight the MacNaughton appears to be a conventional underlever, hammer 12-bore shotgun with bar action locks – very well made but with a minimum of engraving. The lockplates bear the name J. MacNaughton and the name is carried on the rib with the address 26 Hanover St., Edinburgh. MacNaughton moved to this address in 1869 so the gun cannot be earlier than this, and the style would place it in the 1870s rather than earlier. It is when we bring the hammers to half cock and move the underlever forward that at least one of the unusual features of this gun becomes apparent.

As the lever is moved downwards and forward the barrels first slide forward and then drop down, being hinged at the front of the fore-end. This then is one of the interesting "slide forward and drop down actions" which appeared in the mid-nineteenth century. The MacNaughton action was patented 5 July, 1867 and reference is made in the patent to the use of this type of action for the conversion of muzzle loaders to breechloaders. That muzzle loaders were converted to both pin and central-fire breechloaders by the MacNaughton system I have little doubt but I am of the opinion that the example illustrated was built from scratch as a breechloader. However, we know so little about this type of conversion that I cannot be too dogmatic.

Unlike the more common Lancaster and Dougall slide forward and drop down

actions where the hinge pin occupies much the same position on the bar of the action as it does on a simple drop down barrel action, that on the MacNaughton is to be found at the tip of the fore-end. Unlike the more common actions the MacNaughton has four lumps, the front one serving as the hinge with an elongated slot for the hinge pin, the second is a locking lump in the fore-end, the third forms the cam surface against which the lever operates to push forward the barrels and the last, under the breech, hooks into a recess in the body of the action.

The patent mentions that in converting muzzle loaders to breechloaders the lumps can be attached to muzzle-loading barrels by means of soft and hard solder. With a fixed fore-end the body of the action has to extend forward to the front hinge, and to

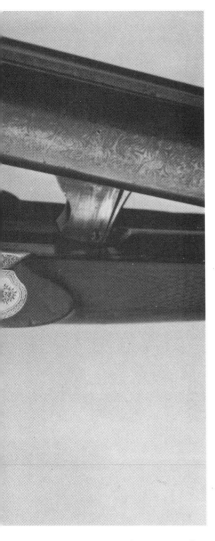

The MacNaughton "slide forwards and drop down action" showing the locking lug or lumps under the barrel.

permit the barrels to be removed entirely from the stock the hinge pin can be withdrawn.

Since all the MacNaughton guns I have seen built on this type of action have been central-fire an extractor is needed. This is operated by a lever on the "camming" lump, and in the illustration where the barrels have moved forward to unlock you can see that the extractor is already partially open.

The operating lever is so arranged that the tail springs over the trigger guard to hold it when the barrels are locked, and an added feature on this gun which I have not seen before is the catch which prevents the triggers being pulled unless the lever is returned fully home. Other features of the gun include the manually operated bar safeties, one for each lock, and the distinctive shape of the hammers.

This was one of the more interesting guns to be seen at the Tayside Field Sports Fair and once again I would like to thank The Angus Gun Room for letting me photograph the MacNaughton and to the organisers for inviting me to the Fair. For me it captured once again the freedom and ease of the early Game Fairs.

THE BACON BREECHLOADER

Bolt-action shotguns, although used in this country, do not enjoy the wide popularity they have in America and in parts of Europe. In America single-barrel bolt-action shotguns by Marlin, Mossberg, Stevens and others still appear to hold their own against single-shot guns with break-open actions possibly because the bolt-action gun provides magazine capacity.

In Europe most of the surviving bolt-action shotguns I have seen in use were old

The slim outline of the Bacon bolt action breechloader is evident here,
but also the extreme length of the action with the bolt open.

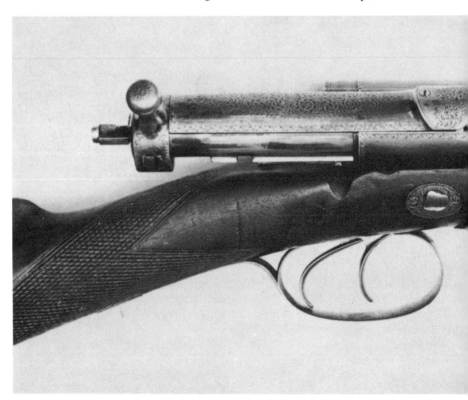

converted military weapons and shared a lineage not dissimilar to our own Martini-action single-barrel shotguns, the earliest of which were conversions from military 0.577/0.450 rifles.

The Bacon enjoyed the distinction of being one of the very few *double-barrel* bolt-action shotguns. To the best of my knowledge I know of none which followed it and but one which preceded it. This was Needham's patent needle gun, also made by Rigby. Two bolts were employed, one for each barrel, but the cartridges differed being "self-consuming", the base wad remaining in the breech after the cartridge had been discharged. The wad was pushed forward when the next cartridge was loaded and those who found the Needham gun superior did so mainly on the basis of the cheaper cartridge and the fact that the fired cases, unlike both pin and central fire cases, did not have to be extracted after firing.

The Bacon breechloader on the other hand fired the conventional centre-fire case and perhaps the only unusual feature of the gun was that the fired case was extracted and removed from the gun through a central slot or hole. The bolt mechanism was patented in 1868 and its application to a double gun was patented in 1870.

The inventor, Lt. Francis Bacon of the Royal Marine Artillery, had but a short service life and went to live with his father who was the Rector of Wymondham near Oakham. Whether or not any single-barrel shotguns or rifles were ever made is still in

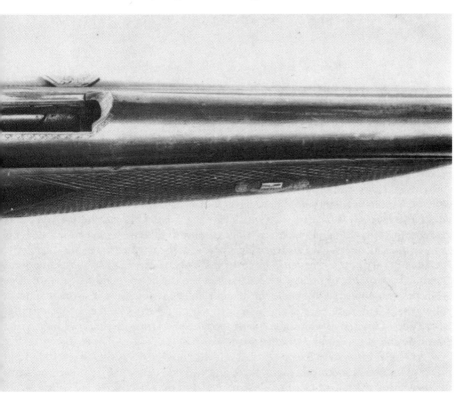

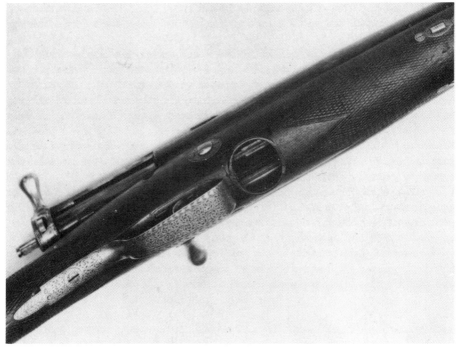

The round ejector port is visible from underneath.

doubt but the double-barrel guns appeared in several variant forms. The example illustrated merely states on the top rib "Bacon's Patent No. 4" and there is no indication where or by whom the gun was made. Quite a few of these unusual guns have survived and the example illustrated was to my knowledge in use twenty years ago. I myself have used an example by Henry of Edinburgh but I doubt that he was the maker. In use I found the gun pleasant to shoot but not as easy to reload as a conventional gun with drop-down barrels and selective ejectors. I cannot compare it with the Needham Rigby since I have never had a cartridge for this gun and although one of its features was the ease with which cartridges could be made for it I have never made any myself, although similar cartridges for use in rifles with external ignition, i.e. capping breechloaders, have had cartridges made for them which have shot splendidly. A contemporary committee on small arms had spoken out against bolt-action guns due to the possibility of premature discharge when the bolt was thrust forward. The inventor, who appeared to handle the promotion of his gun himself, worked hard to popularise it and in defence of the system stated that he had fired over 9000 rounds from a gun of his design without accident and that premature discharge of bolt action guns was due to protruding strikers.

In favour of his system Bacon pointed out that not only was the design sound but that it permitted economical manufacture and was one of the few double gun designs that permitted the reloading of one barrel whilst in the act of firing the other!

Active promotion of the Bacon gun dates from about 1872 and certainly before the end of the decade manufacture had ceased. Few appear to have been used heavily although it can be argued that since not all of the output has survived those which have vanished could well have been worn out!

J. H. Walsh writing in 1882 states that "although the gun is no doubt a strong one it has not taken hold of sportsmen and is now I believe out of the market". This then must be taken as the epitaph of an interesting and unusual gun which, regrettably, never realised the potential envisaged by its inventor and energetic promoter.

PAPE OF NEWCASTLE

In a recent reply to a reader I fell into the old trap of assuming that he had been a subscriber to the *Shooting Times & Country Magazine* for the same amount of time that I had been writing for it. Much of what I write about here can be found in articles written previously for *The Shooting Times*, the earliest going back to 1969.

My keen enquirer was interested in early extraction systems and also how central-fire guns could be made to open in the days before Stanton and his by now famous rebounding lock.

But I'm doing it again – assuming people who have never used a hammer gun will know about rebounding locks. This is something that never bothers the man with a hammerless gun but, in the old days when people fired at game with black powder, long before firearms acts and shotgun licences, guns had hammers which struck against firing pins or strikers to fire the cartridges. The strikers were kept forward by the pressure of the main spring and the tip remained in the indentation in the cap of the cartridge.

This effectively prevented the gun from being opened, and although guns of the previous generation – that is the percussion muzzle loaders – had hammers which could be partially withdrawn to what was known as "half-cock", central-fire guns with similar lockwork would not operate since there was no way of withdrawing the separate strikers from the little dents they had made in the cartridge cap.

All sorts of ingenious devices were thought up by gunmakers of the period to overcome this problem, and in the photograph overleaf you can see one of the dodges thought up by William Pape of Newcastle. His strikers were fitted with hinged levers, one end of which was actuated by the hammer. When this was cocked the lever was also drawn back and it withdrew the striker from the cartridge.

Many schemes were tried. One which has been mentioned in the past was to have the striker attached to the hammer so that when the hammer was drawn back it also pulled back the striker with it. Several similar schemes to the Pape were tried out, a rather neater scheme being adopted by Thomas Horseley of York. It was considerably neater than the Pape idea although the Pape system still works. This is really quite remarkable since the original design dates from 1867, and that is a long time ago!

I don't know when the Pape was made, but it cannot have been very long after 1867 because I have photographs of other Pape guns which have dispensed with the mechanical withdrawal of the strikers (a little coil-spring worked just as well when

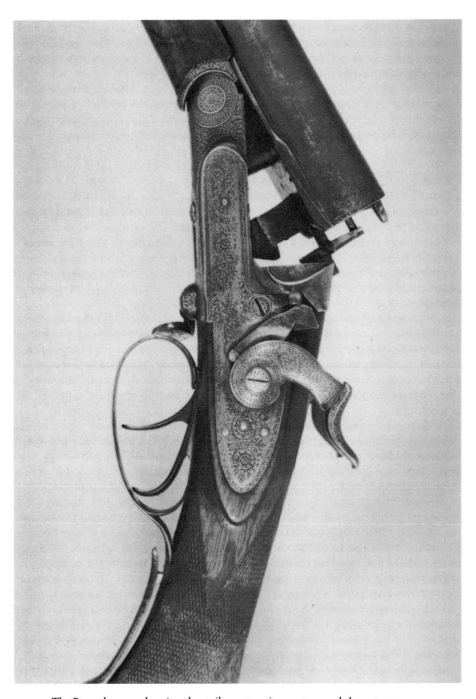

The Pape shotgun showing the striker retraction system and the extractor.

combined with rebounding hammers) but Pape used his extraction system for quite some time after it was patented, again in 1867.

This is a very simple and strong system. The extractor is very similar to the conventional type used today, the little plate with two "legs" or pins parallel to the axis of the barrel. On later extractors one of the pins is used to push the extractor plate forward so permitting the head or heads of the cartridges to be grasped and withdrawn by the fingers. On the Pape gun the extractor plate is not pushed forward but pulled. The plate has a tongue piece, like a doll's head, at the lower edge and this tongue fits into a groove in the vertical breech. When the barrels are opened, the tongue slides up the groove and withdraws the extractor plate and cartridges.

In the illustration the tongue has been moved out of the groove so that its shape can be seen. The Pape abounded with ideas. Another one, the grip safety can be seen in the illustration. This device was recently described and here you see it adapted to a breechloader.

One other feature of the Pape is the fact that it is a snap-action gun. Reload it and close the barrels and the lock snaps shut. On contemporary guns a widely used system was the rotary under-bolt – the English "T" bolt as the French called it. This had to be closed by hand and slightly slowed down the reloading cycle. The Pape has an under-lever, but it is quite short and very easy to use.

It was pleasant to encounter this gun again after a lapse of several years and as with many guns today it was in better condition than when I first saw it. I have complained at the constant increase in the price of guns but at least this increase in value is tending to make certain that many old guns, which might have been placed on the scrap-heap a few years ago, are now more carefully looked after and are treated with respect.

PAPE'S EXTRACTOR SYSTEM

Many years ago I can remember with vivid clarity spending a day shooting with a friend under what were, to me, rather unusual circumstances. The friend was using an old single barrel gun, the extractor of which was broken. Every time a shot was fired the gun was opened and the fired case winkled out of the chamber with a ferocious clasp knife. I was using an ejector gun and felt immensely superior as my fired case flew neatly over my shoulder although I can also remember that my ejector gun didn't make me shoot any better than my friend with his non-extractor.

Today with the increased interest in reloading shotgun cartridges an ejector gun can be more of a hindrance than a help; one eye on the bird and another watching where the fired cases fly to! There is no dispute, however, about the value of an extractor and if one thinks back to the days when pinfire guns were in common use, the fired case had to be prised loose with what must have become rather ragged finger nails. There were one or two pinfire extractor guns but these were the exception rather than the rule.

It was with the appearance of the rimmed central-fire case that extractors became necessary. The earliest of these were not dissimilar to those in use today and that employed by the first British central-fire gun, the Lancaster, employed a plate which was moved rearwards by a linkage attached to the operating rod when the barrels moved forwards before hinging down.

A later Pape lacking the external striker retractors but retaining the extractor system. The channel in the standing breech is shown here in which the "doll's head" extension on the extractor rides.

The breech end of the barrels, with the extractor plate withdrawn to show the construction.

An alternative was the system used by William Rochester Pape for some years. I have no record of the system being used by anyone else but that it was, and is, effective can be verified by the fact that at least two Pape guns with this type of extractor mechanism are still in use.

As Pape puts it, the extractors consist of two "filling pieces" which fit into recesses at the end of the barrels provided with two guide pins parallel to the axes of the barrels. On present day extractors the pins act both as guides and operating rods. On the Pape extractors the system was rather different. The two pins can be seen in the photograph, the large one uppermost, the smaller pin entering the rear of the lump. At the base of the extractor plate is a "tongue" piece, the extension of which slides in a vertical groove in the standing breech. How this system operates can be seen by reference to the second illustration where the extractor extension can be seen at the top of the groove in the breech.

The system is simple, strong and unlikely to go wrong and as at least one of the guns which is still in use is by now past the century I don't think these assertions can be disproved!

THE PURDEY BOLT

If you use a side-by-side top lever double shotgun the chances are that the barrels will be held down by a Purdey bolt. The concept of "drop down" barrels introduced by the Lefaucheux "crutch" gun was ideally suited to sporting shotguns and, although a number of alternative systems were proposed and manufactured, very few have stood the test of time.

When it came to a means whereby the barrels were secured to the action, the ingenuity of the gunmaker was given full rein for, as explained in a previous chapter, the original Lefaucheux locking system was prone to wear loose and, whilst the rotary bolt had much to commend it, the ideal was a "snap" action which reduced to a minimum the effort of the sportsman and considerably speeded up reloading.

The top lever, double-bite, Purdey bolt did not appear overnight; it was one of many systems proposed, all of which attempted the grand desideratum, strength, speed, convenience of operation and a pleasing appearance.

Strength was sought by combining drop down barrels with a sliding forward movement exemplified by the earliest of this type of action, the Dougall. Several other similar types of action appeared but all lacked one important attribute, convenience of operation.

In 1862, two years after the Dougall, the first top lever system appeared, the Westley Richards. The bolts no longer engaged the lumps underneath the barrel, locking was accomplished by a single bolt engaging a top extension, the "doll's head" and, when combined with Purdey's bolt, this was to provide one of the strongest breech actions developed. The Purdey bolt did not appear for another year and, in its original form, was operated by a pivoted lever in front of the trigger guard. The barrel lump was divided into two and at the rear of each "lump", a hook-shaped notch was provided. The lumps were able to enter the bar of the action passing through which is the rectangular bolt. There is a rectangular slot cut into the middle of the bolt through which the rear lump can pass and, when this has happened, the bolt is thrust forward by a spring so that the front edge engages the notch in the front lump and the rear edge of the slot engages the notch in the rear lump. The whole length of the bolt moves in grooves cut into the action body and because of the spring action of the bolt, operation was simple, speedy and, even in its original form, convenient to use.

Its function, which is to hold the barrels down, is performed admirably and the only criticism concerns the amount of metal that must be removed from the bar of the action to accommodate the bolt and, for this reason, the later Purdey bolt was often combined with some type of top extension such as the Westley Richards doll's head.

An intermediate step in the evolution of the perfected Purdey bolt was the Mathews bolt, the invention of a Birmingham gunmaker, which also appeared in 1863. In this action a single bite bolt was operated by a top lever and two years later Scott, also of Birmingham, introduced a double bite bolt with top lever, the final Purdey bolt being introduced in 1867.

In the ten years between 1857 and the introduction of the improved Purdey bolt no less than 56 different types of breech bolting were invented. Many were merely modifications of a previous system and some pursued a line of development which was

The table of the Purdey action. The bolt is seen in its forward position.

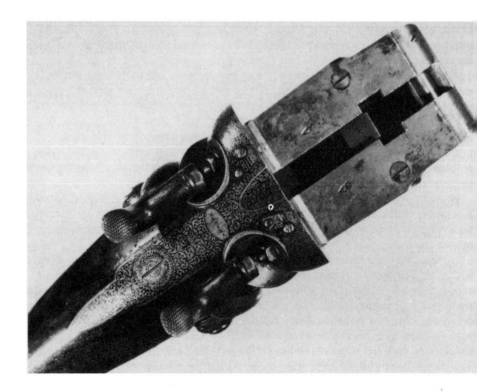

a blind alley in view of later inventions. One such system was that of Law which withdrew the locking bolt when the hammers were placed at half cock. An interesting variant, but one inevitably doomed by the later appearance of "hammerless" actions.

The improved Purdey bolt was, following the expiry of the patent, widely adopted throughout the world. It is to be regretted that Purdey never really received due credit for his remarkable invention which, for the side-by-side double, is almost the universal locking system today.

Many of the "unsuccessful" actions nevertheless gave yeoman service and, from correspondence, many undoubtedly still survive. If you have such an action I would be pleased to have a description. Such guns were used and used and few have survived to grace a museum collection and unless they are recorded now they will be lost forever.

WIGGAN & ELLIOTT SHOTGUN

I wonder how well Eric Wastie of Leys Farm remembers the 1977 Game Fair at Woburn. I remember it as two quite unforgettable days in my life. At the time I took enough photographs to last me a whole year and I have still not used quite a lot of them. Many of the large number of guns that were brought to the Fair for me to see were of high quality and interest value. Eric Wastie's gun was one of the more interesting ones. It had been rebarrelled by Powell's of Carr's Lane, Birmingham, but otherwise it was in very good external condition.

As you can see from the photograph overleaf the gun is a double-barrelled shotgun with bar action hammer locks and an underlever. The locks and the bar of the action are covered with wood and the arrangement of the hammers and strikers is very neat. The nose of the hammer on each lock is turned inwards to allow a good direct blow to the strikers. In later guns the whole of the top of the hammer curves inwards bringing the combs of the hammers closer together.

The name on the lock plate of the gun is Wiggan & Elliott. I didn't know anything about the firm when I first saw the gun and I have to admit that I know very little more now. I do not have any listing for the firm but I imagine that the Wiggan was in fact John Wiggan, for some weeks later I was given a detached lock plate, rather earlier, bearing this name but, again, no address.

The lock plate was given to me by Mr. Walter Willis when I accepted the invitation extended to me at the Game Fair to visit him. Usually one takes a present to one's host but in this case I received a present from my host! The detached lock plate is of good quality and I think it is from a percussion gun. It has one or two unusual features about it, one being the fact that the sear pin enters from the outside of the lock plate and the slotted head can be seen behind the tumbler.

However, back to the Wiggan & Elliott shotgun for this has some surprises in store for us. If the underlever is pushed forward the barrels are released and drop down. One

Overleaf
In the Daw/Schneider gun the locking bolt entered under the barrels. In
the Elliott patent gun as made by Wiggan & Elliott the locking bolt
enters above the barrels.

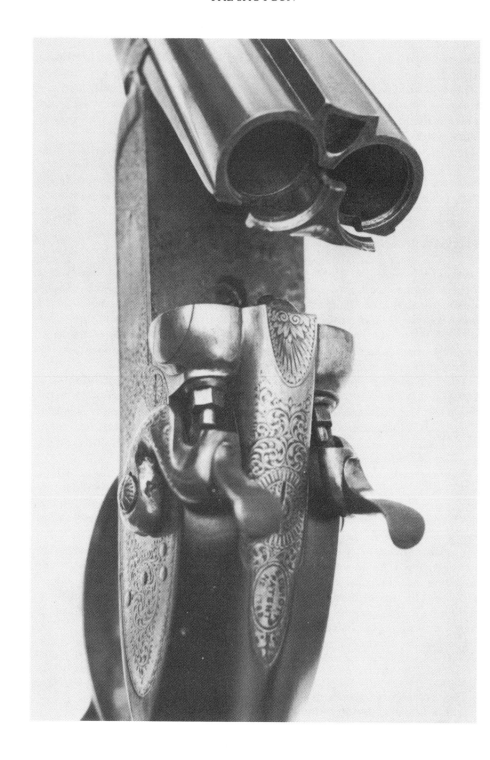

sees from the illustration that there are no lumps under the barrel and no bites for any type of bolts to engage. There is no "doll's head" extension so how is the barrel bolted to the standing breech?

A good question, for this is one of the quite rare bolting systems which actually got off the drawing board or more probably from the chalk sketch on the workshop bench to shaped metal. The patent which covers the design of this early method of breech closure dates from 1863 and was taken out in the name of H. Elliott. Elliott took out only one other patent which dealt with a cartridge extracting tool and I have not been able to discover very much about him. I would guess that Wiggan was the gunmaker, Elliott had the idea and the two of them got together to produce the gun which has survived by delightful chance to intrigue us today.

The original patent drawing shows a vertical lever in front of the trigger guard, the top of which has a curved hook which engages in the top rib of the barrels. In a single barrel gun the top of the barrel would have to be thickened or perhaps the inventor intended the hook to pass over the top of the barrel.

As the lever was pushed forward the top was withdrawn since it was pivoted at the lower end of the standing breech. The hook was withdrawn and the barrels released. In the actual gun made by Wiggan & Elliott some slight changes were made, the lever was altered so that it curved round the trigger guard in a much neater fashion and we see the breech mechanism fitted to a central fire shotgun, not to a pinfire as is shown in the patent.

The design is neat and simple and the gun is well made. One cannot help but wonder if there are other examples which have survived and whether or not other makers made use of the Elliott patent. As it is I am very glad that I have seen this example since it is most rewarding to find actual examples of the patent designs – many no longer exist and many others merely remained experimental designs and have long since been destroyed.

SELF-COCKING HAMMER GUNS

In the second half of the nineteenth century a number of hammer guns were introduced which had the provision for either half or full cocking of the external hammers of conventional double rifles and shotguns. Prominent among those who sold guns and rifles of this type was the firm of Holland & Holland Ltd. The example illustrated overleaf is a double rifle, No. 6423 dating from 1881.

At first sight this is a best-quality double rifle with conventional rotary under-bolt, lever over guard, and back-action locks. The stock has a pistol grip and, as was common with double rifles, the top strap is extended and the barrels have a doll's head extension.

It is at this point that a rather more careful look at the illustration shows that this rifle has a rather unusual feature. At the top of the standing breech, extending to the rare, is a rather odd lever. This can be seen to pass between the two hammers, which are specially adapted to receive the "T" extension of the lever.

The other end of the lever is attached to the barrel lump so that when the barrels are

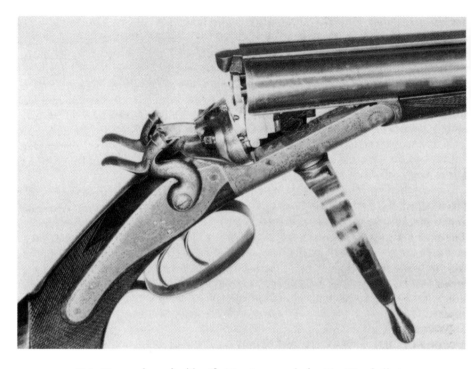

H & H 0.500 bore double rifle No. 6423, made for Mr. Woodville in
1881. Perkes' self-cocking patent.

opened the lever rises and moves rearward, cocking both hammers. When the barrels
are closed and locked the lever returns to the forward position with the "T" extension
flush with the standing breech. From a cursory examination of the rifle when it is
closed with the hammers uncocked, it would be difficult to discover anything unusual.
It is only when the rifle is opened for loading that the self-cocking feature becomes
apparent.

The patent for this type of self-cocking mechanism was taken out by T. Perkes in
1876 and it was one of three variant types, all of which were built by H & H at one time
or another.

Other self-cocking hammer guns were made by Cogswell & Harrison, the patent for
this action being obtained in 1864. The system differed from that described in that the
cocking was done by the underlever and not by the fall of the barrels. Two similar
actions appeared during the 1870s – one by Lang, the other by Woodward. As far as
can be discovered, the Holland & Holland designs appear to have enjoyed the greatest
measure of popular acceptance, the H & H gun being then known as the "Climax",
although it must be remembered that this name was used in later years to describe their
hammerless guns.

I have made an effort to discover a contemporary account of these self-cocking
hammer guns without success. That they enjoyed a certain vogue seems to be likely,

but it is apparent that the added complexity and cost outweighed any positive advantage since self-cocking hammer guns were not made after the introduction of self-cocking hammerless guns although hammer guns of conventional design continue to be made up to the present day.

To what extent self-cocking hammer guns pushed forward the development of the self-cocking hammerless gun is largely a matter of conjecture, but it seems certain that some of the systems which enjoyed their brief popularity must have had some influence on the design of the later hammerless guns, particularly the sidelocks.

PERKES' PATENT SELF-COCKING GUNS

I have already described a very interesting Holland & Holland self-cocking hammer gun in which the hammers were raised to full cock by a bar attached to the barrel lump. The example illustrated was from Holland & Holland's collection and is a .500 black powder express with back-action locks and a rotary underlever. Looking at the rifle with the action closed gives little clue to the fact that here was one of a rather rare breed. Holland & Holland have another self-cocking gun in their collection, a 12-bore side lever double, which dates from 1877 and is four years older than the double 0.55 express.

The "side-pedal" 12-bore has a similar self-cocking action in that the bar which cocks the hammer is attached to the barrel lump. This system is described in Thomas Perkes' patent of 1876 in which he is described as living at 4 Duck Lane, Soho in the county of Middlesex and his occupation is given as gunmaker.

I know little of Thomas Perkes other than his address and occupation. However, his patent describes another system where the bar which cocks the hammers is attached to the underlever. This is the system illustrated. You can see the bar rising from the action bed and passing through the standing breech to emerge between the hammers.

I had no knowledge of the existence of such a gun since both the examples I had seen in the collection of Holland & Holland employed the barrel-cocking system. This is not unusual as very often the patentee will try to cover all possible variations of his basic idea so that someone else coming on to the scene does not manufacture an "improvement" which steals the original idea and obtains the major benefits.

I had hoped that perhaps Mr. Perkes or Holland & Holland had made at least one example of the lever-cocking system, but I was not hopeful since if Holland & Holland didn't have one, my hopes of finding an example were rather slim. Once again, however, I had reckoned without the aid of the readers of my magazine articles. From a Mr. W. H. Smiles came a letter telling me about a Holland & Holland gun he had which was different from the one I had described. Even better, Mr. Smiles was visiting my part of the world and so I would be given the opportunity not only of seeing the gun but also of photographing it. When I had the chance to have a close look at the gun I was delighted to see that it was indeed the alternative Perkes system.

So now we have three variants of the basic patent. The first is the underlever cocking system used on Mr. Smiles' gun, the second the rotary underlever gun with barrel cocking as used by the .500 express, and the third which employs a sidelever instead of the rotary underlever. Possibly there is yet another Perkes Patent gun to be found – one with barrel-cocking and a top lever. I wonder where that one is?

STEPHEN GRANT SIDELEVER

There is a tendency to regard hammer guns as old-fashioned, almost antique weapons and it is forgotten that a great many people continued to use hammer guns long after the hammerless design had been perfected and gained complete acceptance. There is no doubt that the hammerless gun is more convenient to use and is definitely safer since there is not the possibility of a hammer slipping from under the thumb when the gun is being uncocked, resulting in an inadvertent discharge.

The headkeeper of a large estate in Scotland told me how he used to watch the loader for a very famous person draw back both hammers to full cock with the sweep of one thumb. Possibly one of the greatest shots of his day, Earl de Grey, Marquess of Ripon, used a Purdey hammer gun made in 1894 and the Stephen Grant gun is contemporary with the Purdey.

The Grant gun is considered by many to be one of the most attractive game guns ever built. The fine damascus barrels are a joy to behold and one of the more unusual features of this gun, the sidelever, can also be seen.

The name of Stephen Grant will, I suppose, always be associated with this type of lever. Although shown here on a hammer gun, Grant built hammerless side locks using the same system and his best quality "Side-Lock Hammerless Ejector Guns" could be had with either top or side lever operation. The founder of this firm was the managing partner of Boss & Co., and after the death of Thomas Boss he established his own business in 1866. The reputation of the firm was quickly established and in 1889 the style was changed to Stephen Grant & Sons. In 1920 new premises were obtained at 7 Bury Street and in 1925 the old-established firm of Joseph Lang was taken over and the firm traded as Stephen Grant and Joseph Lang Ltd. The subsequent history of the firm is highly complex. A succession of takeovers followed with the passing of the years, resulting in the formation of the company, Atkin, Grant & Lang, who were to be found at 7 Bury Street, St. James's, London S.W.1. However, this company and its successor have now ceased to trade.

Top right
H & H double hammer gun made under Perkes' patents of 1876. This example follows the patent specification for a gun with the cocking lever attached to a lever which opens the gun instead of to the rear lump of the barrel as gun No. 6423.

Bottom right
In the opinion of many, the most elegant sidelever gun of all, the Stephen Grant. Note how the sidelever compliments the curve of the hammer.

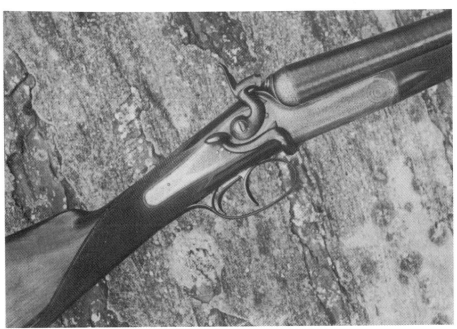

The introduction of the sidelever system is difficult to place with any degree of accuracy since "side levers" of one type or another have been used from the earliest days of breechloaders, for example, the side lever employed by the Dougal "Lockfast", but the type which we associate with Stephen Grant appears to have become popular about 1875 and was used on the Hollis action.

It is, as can be seen, neat and convenient, and those people who have used this type of lever seem to become thoroughly attached to this system of operation.

The other interesting thing about the Stephen Grant hammer gun which is not readily apparent is that it is an ejector. Hammer ejector guns are by no means common. Today hammer guns are usually in the lower price range and on modern guns it is very much cheaper to eliminate the ejectors and keep the cost to a minimum.

The "best" hammer ejector guns of yesteryear were rare in the first place and like all good guns they were used and used and used. Some were looked after and have survived to delight and please those of us who are attracted by grace and beauty. This is a beautiful gun and it well repays close study.

STEPHEN GRANT UNDERLEVER

One of the difficulties which causes frustration and a feeling of impotence when writing about the early sporting breechloaders is the absence of actual examples. As I have mentioned before, shotguns are used and used and used. For the most part a good gun does not lie peacefully in a gun case to grow old gracefully. Many have a hard life and it is no wonder that after possibly three-quarters of a century even the most splendid of guns can be worn out.

There are people who treasure their old guns and it is largely through their care and thoughtfulness that many of our old guns have survived. It is also because of their kindness that I have had the opportunity, during the past few years, of hearing about many of these fine weapons and also of enjoying the very great advantage of having a photograph. One can tell from a letter when a gun is loved. The word love is used advisedly because fine things do arouse emotion. This is not surprising since fine things require more than hard work to create them.

A letter which I received from Mr. S. A. Williams of Newtown, Montgomery, is an example of the fellow feeling which can arise between gun lovers, two people who haven't met and are very probably unlikely to meet. But I certainly feel that I know something about Mr. Williams and that we could get on well together. The story of the Stephen Grant sidelever gun is where the story really starts. Mr. Williams wrote to me and told me that he had a Grant gun which he greatly loved but that it was slightly different to the one mentioned earlier. In course of time I received a photograph of Mr. Williams' gun together with the information that the breech face bore the legend Grant & Hodges Patent No. 146.

It is at this point that we encounter problems because the "No. 146" does not refer to the Patent number which, to add further to the problem, was not taken out by Grant & Hodges anyway but by E. C. Hodges alone in 1871. Edwin Charles Hodges was a London gunmaker who, in 1900, lived in Islington. Whether or not he was in business for himself after working for the firm of Stephen Grant we do not know. The firm known as Atkin, Grant and Lang originally traded as Stephen Grant, a firm established in 1866 by Grant who was formerly the managing partner of Boss & Co.

Little is known of Stephen Grant as a man but he was renowned for building traditional-type sporting guns and rifles of the highest quality. We know even less of Edwin Hodges. His first patent was taken out in 1865 and the one which covers the principle upon which the Grant gun is constructed refers to the locking of the barrels.

The photograph which was kindly provided by Mr. Williams shows the principal feature of the patent. The first of these is the rear extension to the lump. This engages a sliding catch in the centre of the standing breech. This catch can be drawn back by pushing forward the hinged underlever. In addition, there are two projections in the middle of the lump, one on either side. Added locking is provided by the sliding catch having two projecting pins which engage these projections when the catch moves forward under the influence of a spring when the gun is closed. This action is a snap-action since the front face of the catch, which cannot be seen in the photograph, is inclined.

It would not be fair to leave you with the impression that this gun is not used or that Mr. Williams is just a collector of vintage guns. From his letter it is apparent that the

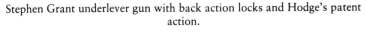

Stephen Grant underlever gun with back action locks and Hodge's patent action.

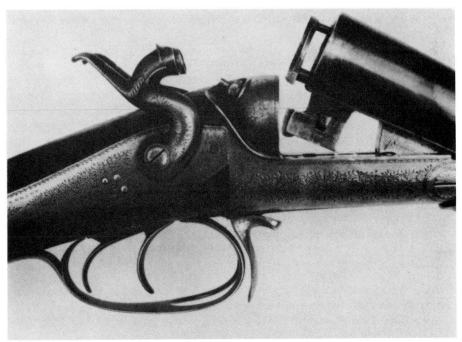

The hammer on an Alex Thomson shotgun. A joy to behold; form and
styling and most tastefully engraved also.

gun is loved, not only for its beauty and elegance but also for the very necessary
functional qualities which, I am told, produce such good results on clay birds at the
Mochdre Gun Club where Stephen Grant's patent gun No. 3453 still exhibits those
desirable qualities which give meaning to the term "best" gun.

HAMMERS

A few years ago I visited an exhibition of hammers. They were not shotgun or rifle hammers, but hammers for slaters, platers, coopers, blacksmiths, bricklayers, joiners and a number of other trades. Each trade had its own special design of hammer and the overall impression was one of suitability for the job coupled with a grace and elegance of outline and form that is associated with articles of functional simplicity. I cannot help thinking about this display of hammers when reading a letter from a Mr. Lewis. Mr. Lewis very kindly sent me some photographs and negatives among which was one of a shotgun hammer. He told me that he had "included a close-up of the Alex Thompson hammer as the workmanship is quite superb".

Now, before you read any further, have a good look at the illustration opposite of the hammer. Look at it really closely. Decide what exactly the hammer has to do. When this is settled see if you can think of a better shape. Have you any other photographs of hammer guns where the hammers are shown clearly enough for you to be able to make a comparison? What is the difference between the hammer shown here and those you have seen in the illustrations previously, in catalogues or in gun books or even the hammers on a hammer-gun that you own?

I have a slight advantage over you since I have a photograph of the entire gun and from this it is quite certain that the hammers are correctly proportioned – that is they are neither too large nor too small in relation to the rest of the gun. This did tend to happen with some of the large-bore hammer breechloaders where the hammers were far too small and this disparity in size destroyed the harmony.

The shape of the hammer should next be considered. It is indeed very graceful. A look at some of the early percussion hammers illustrates that this grace did not arise by accident. Early percussion hammers, particularly those for pellet or pill locks are singularly lacking in charm and, in my opinion, it wasn't until the half century that the percussion hammer became sufficiently attractive to bear comparison with the grace and elegance of its flintlock predecessor.

The styles of percussion hammers were many, and it is the vestiges of such styling that we can trace in the later hammers fitted to guns of the central-fire period. Pinfire hammers were, to some extent, a digression, since the blow had to be downward – not angled as with both the percussion nipple and the central-fire striker. The "S" shape of the hammer is useful to clear the very charming fence around the striker, but, for example, the hammer could have been made as a reversed "C" and still work.

The comb of the hammer is another important feature. It has to be large enough and correctly shaped to avoid the possibility of the thumb slipping in wet or cold weather. The shape of the comb is again of interest and it is quite amusing to compare the size and shape of hammer combs. Hammers, in fact, form one of the most intriguing aspects of firearms design – the changes in shape and style, those dictated by fashion and changes in technology. When we have a hammer, the graceful shape of which is complemented by tasteful decoration, we are able to enjoy something which is a work of art. Just have another look at the hammer on the Thompson shotgun again. It's really quite something isn't it?

CHASSEPOT SHOTGUN

Bolt-action shotguns are not so common, at least in the larger calibres, but this particular example is connected with more history than most and, as a military rifle, it must have been manufactured in the tens of thousands.

Invented by Antoine Alphonse Chassepot, the French Model 1866 rifle figured in one of the classical confrontations in military history, namely the Dreyse needle gun, in the hands of the Prussians, against the Chassepot, in the hands of the French, during the war of 1870–1. Although the French suffered a series of disastrous defeats which culminated in the capitulation of Napoleon III at Sedan, the French defeat was not due to any shortcomings of the Chassepot; in fact, in the opinion of many, it was a better military weapon than its rather older opponent, the Dreyse.

The Chassepot did have defects but, in spite of these, its use during the Franco-Prussian War demonstrated that imperfect breechloaders were much to be preferred to muzzle loaders for military use.

Like the Dreyse, the Chassepot fired a combustible cartridge but in 1874 the French adopted a system which "transformed" the Chassepot into a breechloading rifle which took a centre-fire metallic cartridge. This was the 11 × 59 mm Gras. The original Chassepot rifle was modified to take the Gras cartridge which was the first modern French military cartridge and as the Model 1874 the Gras system proliferated into four variant types – Fusil, Carabine de cavalerie, Carabine de gendarmerie, Mousqueton, and four variants known as the Système 1866–74. In 1878 the original design was further modified to incorporate a tubular magazine under the barrel. This was the Model 1878 Kropatschek, used by the French Navy and which served as the prototype for the Model 1886 Lebel.

Other modifications were carried out in 1880 and rifles so altered bear the mark M.80. The basic Gras design, due to Capitaine Basil Gras of the Depot Central de l'Artillerie, had a decisive influence on first generation bolt-action rifles and the Gras rifle, along with the Remington Rolling Block rifle, again chambered for the 11 mm Gras cartridge, was widely used in the Balkans and throughout French colonial areas.

Many conversions of the Chassepot/Gras were carried out by the gun trade in Birmingham and certainly by the end of the First War large numbers of obsolete Gras rifles had come on to the market and were being converted from 11 mm bolt-action rifles to 12-bore, smooth bore, bolt-action, single shot shotguns. Even earlier the Gras had been offered as a "converted military rifle" and potential purchasers were carefully warned that all "had been carefully selected, and if at all faulty are thrown out". The customer was reassured that "all Actions are Tested, and therefore there is not any danger of them going off unawares".

The Chassepot/Gras illustrated must have been carefully tested since it has survived until today and the number that must still be in use in Europe, Africa and South America is likely to be large.

I suppose that this is the sort of gun that most people would regard with some disdain. It has, however, a truly tremendous history behind it and as such should be treated, like the old soldier it is, with respect and consideration.

The French military Chassepot single rifle converted to 12 bore shotgun
for sporting use.

A PAIR OF LANCASTERS

"What is it worth?" A common enough question and one, bearing in mind the present state of our economy, that is quite understandable. The worth of a gun, or pair of guns, is precisely what one gets for them when offered for sale. Where you sell them, how soon you want the money, or whether you are willing to take something in part exchange, all influence what you will realise in hard cash.

There is, however, another value, what I call the "historical value". In what way does the gun tell us about the period when it was made?

Some time ago Mr. Pengelly wrote to me to say that he had a pair of Charles Lancaster 14-bore shotguns. He went on to say that he had "indulged himself" and had the guns carefully restored and he was so delighted with the end result that he would like to know more about them. They were numbered No. 1 and No. 2 and bore the serial numbers 3119 and 3120. They had 30 in. damascus barrels and were in proof.

From the serial numbers I was able to say that they had been made between 1850 and 1860, nearer to 1860, and from this date and from the illustrations which had been provided I was of the opinion that they were conversions either from pinfire to central-fire or, more likely, from muzzle-loading percussion to central-fire direct.

The reason behind this thinking was that the style of gun was far too late for 1860 and that had the guns been converted from pinfire (since in 1860 they could well have been made as pinfire guns) more residual evidence of their pinfire ancestry would have been noticed. The other clue was the shape of the breech end of the barrels.

I suggested that Mr. Pengelly should write to Mr. D. A. Masters who then held the records of the firm of Charles Lancaster and who did make a search for a moderate fee. A word here about "gunmakers' records". In the unlikely event that they have survived for a century (and this has meant time and money being spent on their preservation) it is quite rare for the records to be available in such a manner as to aid the researcher of today. Shop records were intended to help run a business and the information recorded was for that purpose and so, if all the data you or I would like to see is not there, quite often it was never intended to be. The records were not historical documents assembled by scholars for the future; they were often almost shorthand notes of a business transaction.

In the case of Charles Lancaster we are more fortunate. Care was taken to record not only the original transaction but also to record subsequent events which had a bearing on the life of the gun or guns. This continued until quite recently. Miss Betty Brown, at that time a director of Atkin Grant and Lang (incorporating Charles Lancaster), went to a lot of trouble during the time these records were in her care to add any pertinent data when it became available and, if one is fortunate, then quite a history is there to be read. Some guns, of course, were made "for the shop" and if your gun bears a serial number in certain batches then all that is known about that gun is some indication of when it was sold, possibly as close as the actual year of sale.

The "shorthand" is another matter. In one set of books I have been studying for some time now the guns, not made by the vendor, have a complex code system to identify the maker, the purchase price and the selling price. Whole batches of guns are identified by the letters "RSL". It has taken three months to decide what these three letters mean.

The Lancaster books employ a similar shorthand. The entry for these two guns reads "DCC, 14-bore 31" Brls. 71 degrees. Made for G. Tomline Esq., M.A. This entry, dated 1858 is, at some later date (the date not being recorded) amended by a note – "Converted elsewhere to 14 U.C.F. Dble. grips, oblique strikers, bolt forepart, Birmingham Proof". In 1903 there is a further note "Birmingham Nitro Proof $1\frac{1}{8}$ ozs". In the same ink there is an entry "Sir Wm. Priestley Bart" and a later entry simply states "R. C. Priestley". The present owner has been advised that the records have now been brought up to date by the insertion of the date and his name as owner.

So from the records we have now been able to see what has happened to this pair of guns since they were sold in 1858. We know that the guns were made to order, not bought "off the shelf" but the entry poses certain problems. What does DCC stand for? The belief is that this means "double copper cap". Today a gunmaker's records would be unlikely to include the description "breech-loading", but Charles Lancaster in 1858 would need to describe what type of gun was being sold in greater detail since it could have been a Lancaster "base-fire" or a "pinfire" breechloader or one of several types of percussion muzzle loader.

Lancaster's, like Dickson's of Edinburgh, may well have had an eccentric customer

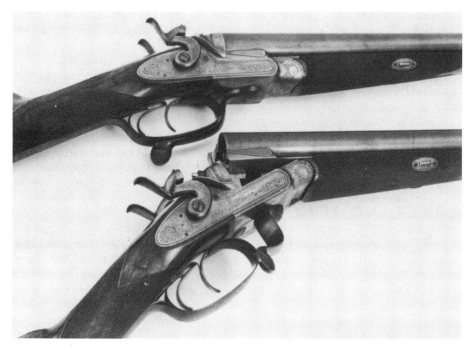

A pair of Lancasters. With rather more history than at first meets the eye
– they deserve a close examination.

who ordered flintlocks even towards the end of the century, though I doubt if there
were many people like Charles Gordon who stands out even in any age of
unconventional characters. Note the barrel length – 31 in. Now they are 30 in. and one
can assume that perhaps the loss of an inch was incurred when the guns were
converted to breechloading. It would have been better for the record if the then owner
had sent the guns back to Lancaster for conversion, but he didn't.

Lancaster's did, however, record that the guns were now "14 U.C.F." – the "U" is a
bit of a puzzle. The "C.F." we can assume to mean central-fire, the "dble grips" refers
to the rotary under-bolt and "oblique strikers" is self explanatory.

The illustration shows the double grip, the inclined or oblique strikers and the "bolt
forepart". This is, of course, the fore-end secured to the barrels by means of a cross-
bolt. The guns must have been satisfactory after their conversion since money was
spent in 1903 having them submitted for nitro proof.

Nothing is known about the owners except that Priestley is possibly the "Squire of
Hazelmere-Bucks" and according to the present owner's researches the estate
gamekeeper was given the guns on his retirement in appreciation of his long and
faithful service. The only remaining clue to the several owners that these guns must
have had during their life is the escutcheon. This is a plain silver oval bearing a crest
and three initials in "black letter". The first two are H.B. and the third could be one of

the following, B.D.H.I. or J. Both "I" and "J" are the same and it is only to be expected that the final letter is the one most worn and the most difficult to decipher but my money would be on I or J.

I wish that only one of the guns had been converted and one left as it was. This would be most useful to see the amount of work done when the gun was converted. It is now nearly a century and a quarter since the Lancasters were first handled by Mr. Tomline. I cannot help but wonder what his feelings were. Did he, I wonder, collect them from 151 New Bond St. or were they, perhaps, delivered? The year 1858 was not exceptional, two years before the Crimean War had been ended by the Treaty of Paris and the Victoria Cross was instituted. In 1857 the Indian Mutiny had started and in 1858 there was a plot to assassinate Napoleon III. Just little political problems!

H. HOLLAND, LONDON

The early history of the present firm of Holland & Holland is slightly obscure. This happens with even the best of "families" and it really means that the researcher (that is me) hasn't been able to collect all the bits and pieces together, thus leaving a few untidy gaps. The earliest gun with the name H. Holland is No. 123. Regrettably there is no record of this gun, nor of the next survivor, No. 304. The first example with any record is No. 641. Mr. Bonham Carter's breechloader. Then we have the first example, No. 1244 which we can date, 1866.

This gun, according to the owner, is a central-fire and this tallies with the record which states "double breechloader, central-fire bar action".

If we go back to No. 123 we are left with some problems. Mr. Heaven, the owner, told me that the gun was not in good condition and he later provided some photographs which clearly show on the bar of the action the words Patent and the numbers 1888 and No. 123. This could, in fact, be 223 and it is not unlikely that this was not even the number of the gun but the number of guns made under the patent which is Patent No. 1888 of 1864. This covers a rather special and unusual underlever

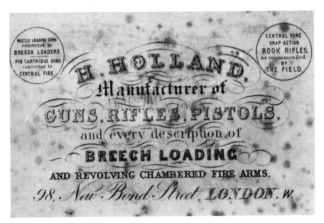

This is an example of the earliest style of H. Holland label. There is no surviving example known of a label bearing the 9 King Street address.

action which was provisionally protected by Redman and Kirkwood. Unfortunately the gun was later converted to central-fire but enough remains of the gun to show that it substantially conforms to the patent.

This appears, at this stage of my researches, to be the earliest breechloader bearing the name Holland. There is doubt as to the serial number since Holland gun No. 592 is dated 1862 although this gun is a percussion muzzle loader. The name on the Redman & Kirkwood gun is Holland and although badly worn it appears the address is 98 New Bond Street, the address to which H. Holland moved in 1860. The firm, incidentally, remained at this address for exactly a century, moving in 1960 to 13 Bruton St. The present firm of Holland & Holland is now located at 33 Bruton Street.

As far as we can tell the first address was 9 King St., Holborn where Harris J. Holland started business in 1835. He was a noted sportsman and a fine shot and he would have been by no means the first sportsman to become engaged in the gun trade.

In May 1858 Henry William Holland was indentured to serve a seven-year apprenticeship and these indentures still survive. When H. W. Holland had served his time he was taken into partnership by his uncle and in 1876 the firm became Holland & Holland, his uncle H. J. Holland retiring in the previous year.

Although Harris J. Holland was not a gunmaker his name is on at least one patent, that taken out in 1861, which covers a hinged and sliding barrel similar to the Dougall lock-fast and perhaps somewhere there is an example of his action still surviving. The Dougall lock-fast was patented in 1860 but at least H. J. Holland was in the forefront of development in those early years of breechloading in Britain. As far as I have been able to discover there are no shotguns bearing the name H. J. Holland although there are some with the name T. Holland and James Holland & Sons who, to the best of my knowledge, have no connection with Harris J. Holland.

As we look at the Holland guns which have survived we see from those for which records exist that Henry Holland was building central-fire breechloaders and of all the examples so far checked the 12-bore was the most popular, only one 10-bore appearing in 1868, No. 1368 and one single rifle No. 3305 made in 1874 in 0.380 C.F. with side snap action. The last Henry Holland recorded by me as still surviving is No. 3493, again a 12-bore but with a top snap lever and rebounding locks.

The label illustrated is the earliest one which has survived and shows the New Bond Street address, so that is post 1860. As can be seen H. Holland were in business to manufacture guns, rifles and pistols "of every description" including breechloaders and those with revolving chambers. Also they would convert your muzzle loader to breechloading and your pinfire to central-fire. There are still a number of gaps in the record but from what we know the firm rested on a sound base and in the years to come was to make a positive and lasting contribution to the development of fine firearms, a contribution which continues to this day.

HOLLAND & HOLLAND PARADOX NO. 15629

With this gun I can bring a little glamour into our lives! The gun illustrated is unusual from a number of aspects: first, it is a hammer ejector; second, it is a "Paradox"; third,

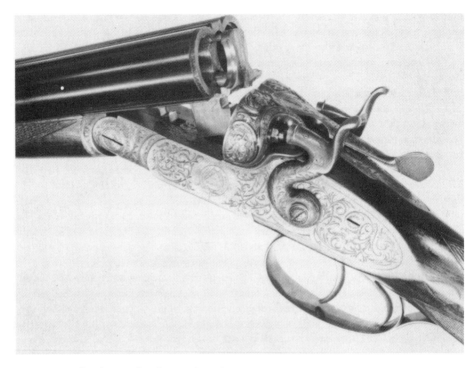

Holland & Holland "Paradox" hammer ejector gun No. 15629. One of a
set of three made in 1903.

it is unusually engraved; and last, it has a known and important provenance.

No, it's not quite "last" for this gun is one of a set of three, a 12-bore "Paradox",
illustrated, a .375 flanged Express double rifle No. 17766 and a 12-bore game gun No.
23259. The firm that made this set of three, Holland & Holland, is so well known that
a history, even a brief one, would appear superfluous.

By the time the gun illustrated was made, in 1903, the firm was well and truly
established as makers of guns and rifles both of which could be truly said to be
"London-made" since the firm had a gun and rifle works in Harrow Road. They also
made a number of significant contributions to the art and practice of gun making. The
12-bore hammer ejector was unusual, for by the turn of the century hammerless guns
were fully accepted and, in fact, the 1910 catalogue does not illustrate even one
hammer gun.

There can be little doubt that the hammer guns were made specially for someone,
who like King George V, preferred to shoot with guns having hammers. This hammer
gun bears the crest of the owner on the lockplate, H.H. the Maharaja of Kolhapur,
who must have had this liking for hammer guns. The owner of this gun, unlike his
illustrious countryman, Prince Victor Duleep Singh, who devoted a great part of his
life to shooting, left little trace of how deeply he was interested in shooting; or at least I

have found little record. So, at this stage, we are left with the knowledge that he liked hammer guns but was not adverse to the march of technical progress since the gun is an ejector.

I mentioned that this was a "Paradox" gun. The invention of Colonel G. V. Fosbery V.C., the "Paradox" was designed to fire shot or a single projectile, either ball or bullet, without loss of pattern with shot, or accuracy with ball. The patent protecting Fosbery's invention is dated 1885 and consisted essentially in rifling or grooving the choke (contracted) portion of the barrels. Fosbery's idea was taken up by H & H and, in 1886, the "Paradox" was tested and the results reported. "Paradox" ball and shotguns were made in 8-, 10-, 12-, 16- and 20-bores and at the sporting ranges then considered customary the accuracy as a rifle compared very favourably with that of a large-bore Express rifle. The pattern as a shotgun compared favourably with that obtained from an improved cylinder shotgun. The "Paradox" gained favour in India and the 10-bore Magnum Nitro "Paradox" was used with success against large game such as elephant.

Although not seen in the illustration the "Paradox" has folded sights for 50 and 100 yards.

All three of the set were hammer guns, including the game gun, and all were marked "Model de Luxe" and had the Bond Street address, the "Paradox" and "Fosbery Patent" inscribed. A hammerless "Model de Luxe" game gun and double rifle were chosen as examples of the finest firearms available at the 1900 Paris Exhibition and these weapons are still to be found in the Museum of Arms in Liège. The engraving is distinctive without being obtrusive.

Each of the three guns is quite outstanding in its own right. As a set of three, they are truly remarkable. As a point of interest the 0.375 double rifle has provision for a telescopic sight, further evidence that the owner was up-to-date in spite of his liking for hammer guns. Finally, of course, the three guns are a splendid tribute to British gunmaking at its best, superb craftsmanship yet with deference to the acceptable eccentricities of a customer who knows just what he wants.

TRACING A GUNMAKER

This is an attempt to tie together several topics which are related to one another by a fascinating gun. One December a day's shooting was kindly arranged for me by my old friend, Allan Paton. We have shot together for nigh on thirty years and, although of late we haven't seen as much of one another as we might, the relationship takes up as smoothly after one week as it does after one or two months. That day went splendidly and all the guns were most concerned about my comfort since unaccustomed exercise plus the aches and pains of advancing years restricted my mobility somewhat.

During lunch I was told by Tom Smith that he had a gun by J. Crawford of Alloa, a town on the River Forth almost within sight of where we were lunching. I had to confess that I did not know the maker and arrangements were made for Allan to bring the gun for me to see at a mutually convenient date. On my return home I looked through the literature and also through my own very complete notes on Scottish gunmakers. To my surprise no J. Crawford was to be found.

This happens rather more often than one might expect, in spite of the number of people who have painstakingly compiled lists of gunmakers over the past century and a half. Whitlaw's book on "Scottish Arms Makers" did not provide any clues and I am left with the gun itself as being the only indication that J. Crawford was in business selling guns in the town of Alloa.

When the gun arrived I was able to examine it closely at my leisure and take some pictures, two of which I reproduce here. You can see that what we have is a bar action, top lever hammer gun with Damascus barrels and what you can't see is that it has a cross bolt and that it is a non-ejector.

A closer look at the gun shows that it is not of "best" quality but is of the type that sold for £10 in the 1920s and more often than not was described by the maker as a "Keeper's Hammer Gun".

It is when we come to the maker that we run into trouble for it is almost certain that this gun was not made by J. Crawford in Alloa but by an unknown maker to the trade in that centre of British gunmaking, Birmingham. Gunmaking in Birmingham was a traditional craft industry and it wasn't until the middle decades of the nineteenth century that it became concentrated about what we today call the "Gun Quarter". This is the area about St. Mary's Church and by 1900 five-sixths of the trade (with the exception of certain specialists such as lockmakers and barrelsmiths) were crowded into a few streets the names of which became known throughout the world.

Even the plainest hammer gun may well have a history and may
contribute something to our knowledge of the past history of gunmaking.
Every gun you came across is worthy of close inspection!

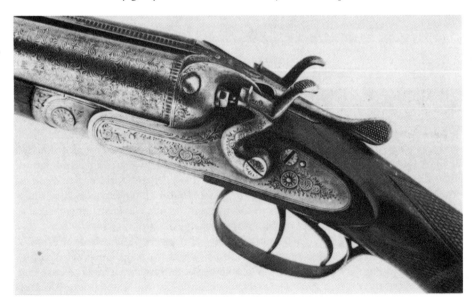

By 1900 there were over 300 firms in the trade, some with names known and widely respected – P. Webley & Sons, W. & C. Scott Ltd., William Powell, Westley Richards, Greener, Isaac Hollis & Sons, Thomas Wild, William Ford, G. E. Lewis and many others. Guns by Greener and others were sold with the maker's style and address "Birmingham" plainly writ for all to see! Other firms never sold a gun with their name on it; either the gun was unmarked or it had the name of the vendor and the vendor's town engraved on lockplate and barrel. This practice was not confined to the small "gunmaker" in the little towns and market places but some well-known names in London had their guns made in Birmingham and it can be amusing to listen to the chap with his "London" gun berating the Birmingham bodgers when his "best" gun, despite its prestige address, was made in the Birmingham Gun Quarter.

Returning to the Crawford gun, this was not made in Alloa but in Birmingham, so let us take it apart to see what else we can find about it.

If we remove the fore-end we see that the gun is a 20-bore and that it bears Birmingham black powder proof marks. The marks date the gun from between 1887 and 1904. However, the most interesting mark is that impressed on the flats of the right barrel. Here we see the marks on a deck of cards, the diamond inside clubs, inside the heart, the whole inside the mark for spades. An interesting mark and one which after a reasonably diligent search I was able to identify as the trade mark of Thomas Wild of Birmingham.

I have been collecting "trade marks" on guns for some years now with very limited success. Some firms such as Webley & Scott ended up with quite a collection. There

Under the barrels one finds the Birmingham proof marks and the very interesting "deck of cards" trade mark.

were the various styles of the Webley "Winged Bullet" and Scott's "Castle" trademark. Ward & Sons of St. Mary's Row, right in the heart of the gun quarter used a "Target" trademark. William Ford also of St. Mary's Row used an "Eclipse" mark on certain grades of gun they made. Greener used his "Elephant" trade mark and, of course, BSA used their "Piled Arms" mark.

From the trade mark on the Crawford gun we know that it was made about eighty years ago by Thomas Wild of Birmingham who worked for many years in Whittall Street and that, in spite of enquiries, the history of the man whose name is so boldly placed on the gun is unknown to us. It is very likely that Mr. Crawford of Alloa was not a gunsmith but an ironmonger and this is why he is not listed amongst the gunmakers though he was a gun vendor.

Thomas Wild continued long into the twentieth century. What is important is that an examination of this gun has shown that no detail, no matter how small, should be overlooked, in our search for information about British gunmakers. So often, the gun is all that remains to us as a record of the life and work of a gunmaker; wood and metal though fragile and subject to rust are more permanent than paper. Where the guns have survived they must be closely scrutinised for any and every clue that will lead us to a better understanding of our gun making heritage.

Index

The figures thus 6 refer to illustrations and captions